ॐ नमं

MW00940190

Creating the Creator

Śrīmad Bhāgavatam's Second Canto

Vraja Kishor

Published January 30th, 2014

ISBN: 1508503990
ISBN-13: 978-1508503996

Contents

Chapter One:

Divinity Without

Cursed to die in seven days, King Parīkṣit renounced his opulent throne and sat on the bank of the Ganges River. Many sages gathered around him, but none could deeply satisfy his spiritual questions until the young man, Śuka, arrived on the scene - naked and without a care for externals. He was the greatest of spiritualists, so the king treated him with great respect and said:

"You are the supreme teacher of all mystics, so I would like to ask you about the ultimate perfection. What is the most important thing to do, not only in normal circumstances but especially when one comes face to face with death?"

The sage was extremely pleased by this question. "O King," he said, "the question you've asked is the very best question! All the learned scholars gathered around you admire and applaud this question."

The king wondered why it was such a good question?

"It is such a good question," the sage said, "because answering it benefits everyone."

One reason the answer to this question benefits everyone is that everyone will die. The king was, from a deeper point of view, not at all the only one who was facing death. But the king wondered why his question would deserve so much applause. It seemed like such a natural question. Wouldn't everyone ask a question like this when they realize they are on the verge of death?

"Very few people ask deep questions," Śuka answered. "Their humanoid minds are completely absorbed in ordinary household chores, obsessed with thousands of mundane topics, and blind to spiritual realities. Their nights are wasted sleeping or spending their vitality like teenagers. Their days are wasted pursuing the endless burden of financial security for their clan. They have no time for anything else!"

The king thought that even such people must become sober when they come face to face with death.

Śuka explained that they ignore death until the very last moment. "They think the health of their unreal body will somehow return; or that their children and loved ones will somehow protect them. They hallucinate that they are surrounded by guardians, and cannot see the destruction and doom closing in on them from all sides." Then, at the last moment, they are paralyzed with terror and shock.

"This is why your question is so glorious," Śuka said. "And the answer to your question releases the soul from all fear and leads to the very best of all topics!"

"Please say clearly, what is the answer to my question: Considering the inevitability of death, what should I do?" the king petitioned.

"The answer to your question," Śuka said, "is this: Do not be like ordinary people. Instead, always absorb your mind in the soul of all souls, the All-Attractive Master, Hari - by hearing and speaking about him."

The king wondered if it could really be so simple; shouldn't he practice yoga, try to comprehend scientific philosophy, or give his last energy to doing good deeds for the world?

Śuka explained that such things are valuable only in so much as they support one's ability to deeply hear and discuss the All-Attractive. "Yogīs, philosophers, and doers of good deeds," he explained, "finally elevate themselves to the most perfect stage when they can always hear about and discuss

Hari. The most important principle for everyone is to always remember All-Attractive Nārāyaṇa, up till the very end."

"What about those who are already elevated," the King asked. "Do they also try to discuss Hari till the very end?"

"O King," Śuka exclaimed, "especially them! Almost all sages fixed in transcendence, above and beyond mere rules and regulations, delight in the spiritual bliss of discussing Hari! I am one example. I was already completely fixed in transcendence, but the unparalleled poetic pastimes of the All-Attractive took hold of my heart. That is why I studied this spiritual treatise, The Beautiful Tales of the All-Attractive, from my father, Island-born Vyāsa."

"I want to hear those Beautiful Tales!" The King spontaneously exclaimed.

"Yes!" Śuka responded, "You deserve to! I will recite those very Tales unto you! If you give your heart to listening, you should very quickly find your thoughts fastened to the Lotus-Faced-Liberator."

The king asked, "What is the central message of these Tales?"

"The essential message of these Beautiful Tales," Śuka explained, "is this: There is no doubt that Hari-Nāma-Saṁkīrtana[1] is the path to fearlessness for everyone and anyone - the desirous and the desireless, the sages and the worldly alike."

AN EIGHT-STEP PATH

The king was overjoyed, but had a worry. "I have little time left to live, less than seven days," he said. "Is that enough to traverse this path to fearlessness?"

Śuka replied with bold confidence, "Time is not an issue! What's the use of meandering through bewildered year after

[1] Enthusiastic glorification of Hari's name, etc.

bewildered year? It's better to be wide awake for even a moment, if in that moment you strive for your true self-interest. The philosopher-king Khaṭvāṅga learned that he would die in a moment, and in that moment he cast off everything and fearlessly attained Hari. You have seven days, much more than he had, so you can take your time and perform everything in a systematic, step by step manner."

"What is the system?" the king asked. "What are the steps?"

The king wanted to know how hear about, speak about and remember Hari in a systematic, step by step manner.

"When the end approaches," Śuka said, "take the blade of dispassion and bravely sever all ties to anything associated with your bodily existence. Leave hearth and home behind and begin the eightfold process."[2]

Śuka explained the eight steps:

Adopt a disciplined and sober character.

Purify your body by bathing at a pure and sacred place.

Sit firmly in a proper place.

Learn to control your breath while remembering the three-letter seed-word, auṁ. This will begin to purify your mind.

Withdraw your eyes and other senses from the external world, using intelligence to focus your attention inward. Then, immediately proceed to the next step.

Fix your mind upon the most auspicious goal.

Focus ever more deeply and attentively upon Viṣṇu's form, keeping your mind vacated of all other desires and objectives.

Finally, you will attain complete satisfaction by dwelling wholly on the supreme platform of Viṣṇu.

---

[2] *Aṣṭāṅga-yoga*

Śuka explained that passion will always agitate the mind to wander, and lethargy will always dull and lull it into sleepy daydreams. By the devotional struggle to hold our mind steadily upon Viṣṇu will gradually drain the power of these effects, and we can then quickly succeed in yoga and witness the most beautifully auspicious repose.

Panentheistic Vision of a Divine Universe

Since it's not easy for everyone to concentrate directly on Viṣṇu, the king asked if there is some preliminary subject to concentrate on first - which would purify the mind and make it more capable of focusing on Viṣṇu.

Śuka replied that one could follow the same preliminary steps he had just outlined - good behavior, proper sitting posture, steady breathing, withdrawal of concentration from ordinary things, etc. Then, instead of focusing directly on Viṣṇu, one could focus on a more basic form of divinity: the form of the All-Attractive that is readily manifest in the tangible world.

He explained why this form of divinity is, at first, easier to contemplate than Viṣṇu: "It is a very tangible embodiment of divinity, well known within everyone's experience. It is in fact more tangible than the most tangible thing, for everything we can possibly experience in the past, present or future is within it. The brilliant embodiment of the Supreme Person within this seven-shelled universe is the initial form of the All-Attractive that the mind must dwell on to purify itself."

Currently, we see the world as an arena full of objects and situations that could potentially serve our needs and fulfill our desires. If we learn to instead see the world as a form of divinity, we will not be inclined to exploit it for our own ends, but will instead develop a humbler attitude of respect and service towards it. This is how awareness of divinity in the natural world purifies the selfish inclinations that distract the mind from more direct meditation.

King Parīkṣit asked, "Please describe how to see this divine form. How can I see this world as a form of divinity?"

The sage explained that there are many metaphors appropriate for viewing this world in a divine light. He began to define a few of them.

Fourteen Realms

Śuka explained that the fourteen levels of reality in the universe can be thought of as fourteen areas of the divine body, the lower levels being the lower parts, the higher levels being the higher parts.[3]

Gods and Elements

Another system is to conceive of the gods and elements of nature as the limbs of the divine body:

Indra and the administrative gods are his arms. The directions are his ears, and sound is his sense of hearing. The twins are his nostrils, and fragrance is his sense of smell. Blazing fire is his mouth, water is his palate, and flavor is his tongue. Dawn is his eyelid, the sun his eye, and illumination is his vision. The supreme controllers and the cycles of the Sun are the movements of his eyebrows. Vedic hymns are his head.

Illusion is his all-intoxicating smile, which reveals his teeth. His front teeth are attachments and affections. They lead to his rear teeth: the god of death. Covering these teeth are his lips: modesty. Powering them is his jaw: greed.[4]

His chest is morality. Immorality is his back. Brahmā the forefather is his penis. His testicles are Mitrā-Varuṇa.

---

[3] *Pātāla* is the soles of his feet; *Rasātala,* his heels; *Mahātala,* his ankles; *Talātala,* his lower legs; *Sutala,* his knees; *Vitala* and *Atala,* his thighs; *Mahītala* (human reality), his hips, Space, his abdomen; The heavenly lights, his chest; *Mahar,* his neck; *Janas,* his face; *Tapas,* his forehead; *Satya,* his thousand heads.

[4] The twins: Aśvinī. Blazing fire: Agñi. Illusion: Māyā. Death: Yama.

Nature

Perhaps the simplest way to conceive of the Divine Universe is to see the basic features of nature as various parts of Viṣṇu's form:

Oceans are his abdomen. Mountains are his bones. Rivers are his veins. Flora are the hairs on his body. The air is his infinitely powerful breath. Rainclouds are the hair on his head. Twilight is his clothing. Time is his gait, and his deeds are the flow of material energy. The singularity is his heart and mind, the wellspring of all things. Matter itself is simply his power of cognition. All beings are simply his will.

Creatures

Various living creatures can also be seen to represent various parts of the Divine Universe: Domestic animals are his fingernails. Wild animals are his loins. The song birds are his artistry. Manu, the forefather of humanity represents his creative imagination. But his mastery of music is reflected only by the heavenly musicians and dancers. The hordes of demons represent his raw power.[5]

Humans

Various types of people can also be seen as analogous to various parts of the Divine Universe: Thinkers are his mouth. Leaders are his arms. Entrepreneurs are his thighs. Workers are in the shelter of his feet.[6]

All people of all ranks and variety should be seen as the devotees of this Universal Form, worshipping him with great endeavor and many treasures.

After saying all this Śuka paused. "This is my explanation," he said, "of the tangible form of my master, Viṣṇu. It is quite easy and natural to concentrate on, because there is nothing else in this world except that form. So,

[5] Human beings are particularly creative and imaginative, but the Gandharva, Vidyādhara, Cāraṇa, and Apsara species excel humans in musical and theatrical creativity.

[6] These four are brāhmaṇa, kṣatriya, vaiṣya and śūdra, respectively.

concentrate all your thoughts upon he who creates all things just like you yourself do in dreams. This will allow you to develop affection and love for the true ocean of bliss. Do not let your thoughts remain affixed to anything else - for that will degrade your heart."

Śuka then cited Brahmā as an example of the purifying power of the Universal Form. Brahmā was completely alone in the universe because he was the first, self-born entity. There was no teacher from whom Brahmā could get knowledge. But by contemplating the Universal Form Brahmā gained clarity and knowledge, and could then recreate the world exactly as it had been before the destruction.[7]

[7] In the original Sanskrit, this paragraph is the first śloka of the Second Chapter.

Chapter Two:

Divinity Within

Śuka intended to explain more about Brahmā, but that would have to wait. Among the audience of sages gathered around King Parīkṣit one stood up to ask a question. "You have advised this dying man to meditate on Hari, beginning by contemplating his Universal Form. You say that spiritual knowledge will result from this, but wouldn't it be more practical to get such knowledge by studying the Veda directly?"

Śuka looked carefully into the eyes of this sage and replied, essentially, that the Veda is too confusing. "We hear and recite the Vedas," he said, "and so many mantras pass into and out of our minds - so many words come into our thoughts... but what do we grasp? If we don't really understand those words, our brains simply wander through a maze of verbiage, like a man wandering through dreams."

Then another sage stood up and voiced a doubt. "This man is about to die. Shouldn't you instruct him how to perform the rituals necessary to enter paradise in the afterlife?"

Śuka was not at all impressed with this question. "That's not a very good suggestion at all," he said. "It would distract him towards useless things."

"Paradise is useless?" the doubtful sage asked.

Śuka was as calm as he was firm. "Yes, useless. There is nothing real about heaven! It is just another illusion. You cannot obtain real treasure by adventuring in a dream. We should indulge the temptation to interact with dreamlike names and objects only as much as absolutely necessary. Otherwise we wind up sucked into a whirlpool of meaningless hard work. People who are experienced, sober, and resolute are fully aware of this."

King Parīkṣit wanted to know what Śuka meant by absolutely necessary. How much interaction with worldly things is "absolutely necessary"?

Śuka explained: "You have the ground, so why struggle to get a bed? You have your arms, so why work for a pillow? You have hands, so do you really need forks and knives? You have the four directions or the bark of trees, so do you really need nice clothes?"

Of course, not everyone can live at this level of simplicity but those who are sages seriously striving for spiritual accomplishment should. So Śuka rhetorically asked, "What sort of 'learned sage' flatters those who are intoxicated with wealth!? Why should a sage beg? Why beg for clothing - can we not find old clothes discarded on the road? Why beg for amenities - have the rivers dried up? Why beg for shelter - don't the trees already put a roof over our heads? Have the caves closed? Does the Unconquerable no longer shelter his devotee???"

The Divinity Within

"I understand," the king said, "that meditating on the Universal Form will purify my thoughts so that I can advance further in my meditation on Hari. So, what is the next step after becoming somewhat purified by learning to perceive divinity within the universe?"

"When your mind is purified by contemplating the Universal Form," Śuka said, "you can then successfully turn your concentration towards the eternal treasure, the Limitless All-Attractive Beloved-of-your-Soul, who is perfectly situated within your consciousness by his own will. Becoming affectionate towards him will liberate you by terminating the very cause of your entanglement in repeated birth and death."

The king asked if the spartan simplicity Śuka had just described was a prerequisite for this meditation.

Śuka affirmed that it was, indeed. For the complications that arise from pursuing material comforts are a serious distraction from meditation. "Materialists are so distracted," he explained, "that they can't focus upon the All-Attractive. Like animals, they pursue unreal objects, even though it is so laborious. The River Styx[8] springs from their hard work and drowns them in misery."

The king had only seven days to live, and so had abandoned all material interests. He was ready to practice this meditation, so he asked how it should be done.

Śuka submerged into a sublime bliss as he told the king to Contemplate the All-Attractive Person by envisioning him within one's own consciousness, especially in the hand's-width region of the heart. We should envision...

His four hands - carrying a lotus flower, wheel, conch, and club;

His smiling mouth;

His eyes like lotus petals;

His clothes the yellow of Kadamba pollen.

His lotus-like feet reclining upon the lotus-whorl of our mystically awakened hearts;

Precious jewels effulgently decorating his limbs as they dangle from golden ornaments on his crown and earrings; A golden streak on his chest; The Kaustubha jewel hanging on a golden chain from his shoulders, next to a beautifully fresh necklace of forest flowers; A gorgeous belt, very valuable rings, ankle bells, bracelets and so on.

---

[8] Vaitaraṇī River

His thick, spotless, shiny, curling, blue-black hair...

His delightful face and charming smile expressing kindness...

His dancing eyebrows expressing affection.

Śuka broke his own meditation to peer towards the King. "First," he said, "you must make a deliberate effort to concentrate on this form of the Master. But if you do so, soon your mind will very naturally fixate upon him. Concentrate systematically on each limb of Viṣṇu's beautiful form, beginning from the feet and ending with his smiling face. As you fully conceive of each limb, your contemplations will become purified and naturally your meditation will progress higher and higher."

Then Śuka gazed at the sages gathered around the king, some of whom were inclined towards materialistic rituals, and others who were inclined towards the externals of education. Towards them, he said, "Do not even begin this process until you have developed a devotional link with the Enjoyer of Matter and Spirit. Until that time, carry out your moral responsibilities and concentrate upon the tangible pantheistic form of divinity we previously described."

Meditation at the Time of Death

Since he was going to die in seven days, the king wanted to know how this type of meditation would work when the meditator was on the verge of death.

Śuka explained that at the time of death such meditators renounce everything in a peaceful mood. They don't worry about anything, not even whether or not it is a proper time and place to die, nor do they regret having to give up their body - which they see as simply a worldly appendage to their true selves. They simply sit down, firmly and comfortably, and take full control of how their consciousness and emotions flow through their breath towards their senses.

“How do they manage to control their emotions at such an intense moment?” the king asked.

“Their pure intellect forcefully absorbs their emotional mind.” Śuka explained, “Then, the conscious entity who witnesses the mind and intellect absorbs them both. Finally, this contracted individual entity compacts itself within the source of itself. Thus the individual attains absolute focus and peace, and ceases from all extraneous enterprises.”

“Do they ever become distracted?” the king asked.

“Not even the gods can distract them,” Śuka replied. “Not even fate itself, the master of the gods, can distract them. They are completely freed from every influence of material energy: clarity, passion, and ignorance. They are beyond the transformations proceeding from the originating singularities and primordial states.”

“You said they attain absolute focus,” the king inquired. “What do they focus on?”

“They focus on full awareness of Viṣṇu’s supreme position,” Śuka answered.

The king asked, “They have no other interest at all?”

“They examined everything in this world and decided, ‘This isn’t what I’m looking for, neither is that.’ They want to rid themselves of all such anxiety-laden nonessentials. Their sweet hearts are exclusively devoted, at each and every moment, to embracing the only object in which they find true value: Viṣṇu’s feet.”

“How do they exit their body at the time of death?” asked the king.

“They completely retire from the world when their realized vision of philosophical imports has become extremely powerful,” Śuka said. “Then, they sit with their heel blocking the anus so that they can raise the life-air through six stations.[9]

"Thoughtfully, these wise souls use the rising vital airs to lead their consciousness from its point of origin to the navel, then into the core, then to the chest, and gradually into root of the palate. Finally, they lead their consciousness between their eyebrows and close all the seven bodily outlets completely. Existing for half a moment in this independent state, they set their sights upon Viṣṇu's worry-less position and cast off their body by bursting out through the top of the head, towards that supreme destination."

THE AFTERLIFE OF A YOGĪ

"What happens next?" the king eagerly asked.

Śuka explained that if they still have personal ambitions they will be detoured from their ultimate goal. On the way towards the supreme they might want to use their mind and sensual faculties to enjoy the multifaceted world as supernatural beings who have eight mystic powers.

King Parīkṣit was a little dismayed. He asked, "Is this attainment any different than the paradisiac goal achieved by rituals and responsibilities?"

Śuka explained that it certainly was. "Those who have cultivated knowledge, austerity, yoga, and meditation," he said, "can attain material destinations without being limited to them. They continue to progress within and beyond these destinations in a purified, subtle body. Those who perform the rituals and responsibilities of karma cannot attain such perfection."

The king asked, "What is the complete path they can travel?"

---

[9] "Life air" is the medium transmitting consciousness to the physical realm. So "raising the life-air" amounts to raising the focus of consciousness. "Six stations" refer to the six "chakras." The yogi exits the body through the seventh chakra.

"First, they traverse the path of space to reach the heavens of the Sun," Śuka said. "When they can progress further on the path towards Brahmā, they follow the Sun's ray towards to Moon. When they are completely pure, they move upwards into Hari's circle of stars. Amongst all of them who enter that circle stars, perhaps one will be pure enough to continue onward and enter the naval of the universe, the place where worshipable beings with vast knowledge enjoy extremely long lifespans."[10]

"How long does the yogi remain in the naval of the universe?" The king asked.

"At most," Śuka answered, "until he sees that the blazing fire from the mouths of the celestial dragon, Ananta, has become an inferno consuming the universe."

"What does he do then?" The king asked, with great interest.

"He flees still higher," Śuka replied, "to the abode of the supreme material being, Brahmā."

"How does he get from the naval of the universe to Brahmā's abode?" the king asked.

"By a technology that only the masters of perfection understand." Śuka answered.

"How long can he stay there?" the king asked.

"At most," Śuka replied, "for as long as the universe exists."

"Brahmā's abode is the highest realm in the universe," the king said. "What is it like?"

"There is no grief," Śuka said, "nor death, nor old age, nor pains, nor anxieties. Except sometimes... sometimes there is anxiety in the heart."

Parīkṣit was amazed, "Why?" he asked.

---

[10] The "ray" linking the Sun and Moon is *Suṣumṇa.* The path linking the Moon to the circle of stars is *Śiśumāra*. The "navel of the universe" is the abdomen, the central, interior, original portion.

“The citizens of that abode are extremely compassionate,” Śuka explained, “they feel anxiety out of sympathy for those who have no idea how to escape from the miseries that they experience again and again in life after life.”

The king was pleased to hear this, but he knew that the yogī’s original aim was even higher. So he inquired still further, “This is the highest realm in the universe, so where can he go from here?”

“Now he begins to leave the universe,” Śuka explained. “He begins his journey through the gigantic universal shells of primordial earth, water, fire, air and ether.”

“Won’t he be destroyed by these raw, primordial elements?” the king asked.

“No,” Śuka said. “He himself takes elemental form to move through these layers as a light wave.”

The king wanted to know what the yogī encounters in these universal shells. Śuka explained that each shell is a primordial templates of the substance required for sensual perception. In the layer of earth the yogī experiences the primeval form of aroma, and thus surpasses the need for the sense of smell. Then he can enter the layer of water where he tastes the primordial flavor, and can thus surpass the need for the sense of taste. Then he can enter the layer of fire and see the primordial beauty, thus rising beyond the need for further use of the sense of sight. Then he can enter the layer of air and feel the primordial touch, thus rising beyond further need for the sense of touch. Then he can enter the layer of ether and experience the primordial template of sound, thus eliminating any further need for the sense of hearing. Thus the yogī exhausts all material desires.

“What happens next?” the king raptly asked.

“Then he can enter the next layer.” Śuka briefly replied.

“What layer is that?”

“It is the layer of ego,” Śuka replied, “the substance from which all sequences start.”

"What happens to him there?"

"When he enters this layer," Śuka said, "the elemental templates of sense perception which he has compacted in the previous five layers will merge into ego, along with their desires and destinies."

"What is the final layer?" the king asked.

"The next and final layer is the source of knowledge," Śuka replied. "If he enters this, his ego will merge into it, completely annihilating his ties to the three qualities of material existence."

"What then?"

"Liberation," Śuka declared. "That completely pure soul can finally enter the soul of the soul and attain peace and bliss. Indeed he can taste the infinite limits of bliss! The person who attains this All-Attractive destination certainly never again consorts with this lowly place, O King."

How Do You Know That?

Śuka could see that the king was amazed by his exact and detailed explanation of the yogī's path through the afterlife to liberation. So he reassured the king, "The answer I've given to your excellent question is an eternal principle spoken of in the Veda."

"But how does the Veda know of such things?" the king wondered.

"Because the Veda originates from the teaching of Brahmā, the creator," Śuka explained.

"But you've spoken of things outside the universe and beyond the creation," the king wondered. "How does Brahmā know of such things?"

"Because the All-Attractive Son of Vasudeva was pleased to explain these things to him in ancient times," Śuka explained.

"Why was the All-Attractive pleased to explain transcendental secrets to Brahmā?" asked the king.

"Because of Brahmā's pure devotion," explained Śuka. "As you wander through this world, you will find no path more auspicious than bhakti-yoga - the path of pure devotion, which links your heart to the All-Attractive Son of Vasudeva."

"Did Brahmā make the importance of bhakti-yoga clear, in the Veda he taught?" The king asked.

"Yes, but to make it more clear, the All-Attractive became a sage who scrutinized Brahmā's Veda three times, clarifying it each time to more conclusively establish the exalted position of divine love."[11]

The king was delighted to hear this, and asked, "These yogīs you just previously described, do they also practice bhakti-yoga?"

"Yes," Śuka answered. "In their own way, befitting their own nature."

The king asked for more detail.

"Meditative yogīs experience All-Attractive Hari by his quality - the quality of sentience - present within the core of all living beings," Śuka explained. "They know they are sentient - they can see, experience, and comprehend. Sentience, consciousness, is a divine thing - an energy of Hari. So, by experiencing their own consciousness they experience Hari within themselves. Further, they perceive that everything they are conscious of also possesses some degree of consciousness. Thus they inferentially experience the All-Attractive divine everywhere."

---

[11] Hari delivered Vedic knowledge to the heart of Brahmā, and Brahmā disseminated this knowledge through the world by teaching it to his children. However, the All-Attractive periodically empowers a sage, Vyāsa, to scrutinize all these teachings and make them more simple and clear. Vyāsa's first review produced the four Veda. The second produced the Upaniṣadas. The third produced the Purāṇas. Thereafter Vyāsa clearly and firmly established the ultimate conclusion of Vedic knowledge in his final work, Śrīmad Bhāgavatam (The Beautiful Tales of the All-Attractive).

Since Hari is the essence of all realization, Śuka emphatically said, "Therefore all people, in all places, all circumstances, and all times should wholeheartedly hear about, glorify, and remember the All-Attractive! That's my answer to your question of what an intelligent human being should do when faced with death."

Chapter Three: The Purpose of Mundane Religion

Śuka had declared that hearing and chanting about Hari was the most important human activity. Several sages doubted this answer, considering it one-sided and biased to say that one only needs to worship Hari and nothing else is very important. Śuka addressed them in an unusual tone of voice, as he began reciting a long list.

"If you desire the spiritual light, worship those who protect spiritual knowledge," he said. "If you desire virile senses, worship the king of paradise. If you desire children, worship the progenitors. If you desire opulence, worship the goddess of illusion. For power, worship fire. For wealth, worship the gods of tangible things. For bravery, worship the mighty gods of destruction. If you want food, worship the mother of the gods. If you want to enjoy heaven, worship her children. If you want career recognition, worship everyone. To be prosperous in business, worship the gods of success. To be healthy, worship the twin gods of health. For sustenance, worship the earth. For stability, worship the horizon. If you want beauty, worship the celestial musicians. If you desire beautiful women, worship the celestial courtesan. If you desire power over everyone, worship the supreme material being. If you desire fame, worship sacrifice. If you want riches, worship the clever gods of wealth. If you want knowledge, worship the god who became transformed by knowledge, Śiva. If you want an excellent marriage, worship his most exemplary wife: Satī. If you desire morality, worship the most renowned Viṣṇu. To protect your family, worship the ancestors. To secure safety, worship moral people. To become strong, worship the winds. To become a king, worship kings. If you want to destroy, worship the goddess of lies. If you desire pleasure, worship intoxication.[12]

"But if you desire to be free from desires," Śuka concluded, "worship the Supreme Being."

He looked at king Parīkṣit as if encouraging him to ask the obvious question. The king asked, "Then we shouldn't worship the Supreme Person unless we don't want anything at all?"

Dramatically changing his tone of voice, Śuka opened his eyes wide and announced, "Anyone with a truly open mind knows that the Supreme Person should be adored by everyone, for all reasons, and in all circumstances! Maybe you desire nothing. Maybe you desire everything. Or maybe you desire liberation. Regardless of what you desire, be wise and worship the Supreme Person with a very strong bond of love!"

WHY WORSHIP OTHER GODS?

The king asked, "Then what's the point of the long list you just quoted? Is there any circumstance in which we should worship the gods instead of expressing devotion to Hari?"

Śuka explained that, "Sages and scriptures encourage worldly people to fulfill their mundane ambitions by worshipping the gods because when they become involved in worship, they start to deal with priests - people who have

---

[12] Names of the divinities, respectively, Brahmāṇa-pati (teachers), Indra, Prajāpati, Māyā-devī, Agñi, Vasu, Rudra, Aditi, Āditya, Viśvadeva, Sādhya, Aśvini, Ilām, Gandharva, Urvaśī, Brahmā, Yajña, The pracetas headed by Varuṇa, Śiva, Umā-Satī, Uttama-śloka, Pitṛ, Puṇya-jana, Marut , Manu, Nirṛti, Soma.

read scripture carefully. The more they deal with such people, the more likely they are to encounter a rare soul who actually understands the sacred texts. The more they encounter such souls, the better their chances of coming into the company of devotees of the All-Attractive. When that finally happens, they can attain the supreme benediction: unwavering heartfelt affection for the All-Attractive."

The king expressed a doubt: "If they are materialistic why would they be much interested in hearing from the wise and the devoted even when they finally meet such rare people."

"When one performs the duties of worship," Śuka replied, "one invariably becomes more responsible and less selfish. Thus the incessantly swirling waves of materialism begin to subside and spiritual knowledge begins to arise, along with a perception of self-satisfaction. This is why religion, even in a mundane form, is the masses' tried-and-true path towards annihilating the self-centered ego and gaining an opportunity to develop the link of selfless devotion. When one becomes purified by the duties of religion, it becomes very difficult not to develop heartfelt affection for discussing Hari."

Hungry for More

Śaunaka was amazed to hear Sūta narrate this discussion between Śuka and the king. When he heard Śuka confirm the exalted position of discussions about Hari, he stood up enthusiastically and declared his own desire to hear more about All-Attractive Hari. He asked, "What other questions did the King have for Vyāsa's poetic and sagacious son, after hearing this extremely perfect answer to his original question?"

"They discussed many things," Sūta replied, "are you sure you want to hear them all?" Sūta knew that Śaunaka was completely dedicated to hearing about the All-Attractive, but he subtly questioned if the rest of the assembled sages were of the same mind.

"O learned Sūta," Śaunaka said in a pained voice. "Are we not listening to you very carefully? It is only right that you continue speaking to us! "

"Perhaps not all of what they discussed," Sūta said, "is directly about Hari..."

"No, no," Śaunaka replied, "The sage and the king were both very saintly. Therefore everything they discussed would certainly, inexorably lead to Hari - for discussion of Hari is the constant anchor of the saintly!"

"But the king was a warrior," Sūta tested.

"Though a warrior, he was a Pāṇḍava!" Śaunaka replied. "He was certainly a great devotee. Even as a child, he would reenact Krishna's pastimes with his toys. As for the sage, the blessed son of Vyāsa was also completely dedicated to Vasudeva's Son. The two, Parīkṣit and Śuka, were great souls. When great souls speak, the discussion must certainly rise to the topic of Krishna!"

Sūta looked out at all the sages gathered around him. Perhaps they were not eager to continue listening? "We've been talking for a long time already," he said. "Maybe we should take a break first, and return tomorrow to discuss these things?"

Śaunaka replied, "The Sun rises and then sets, stealing the moments of our lives. But a moment spent discussing the Subject of Topmost Poetry cannot be stolen away!" A single moment of hearing about Krishna is more valuable than years and years of ordinary life, so what is the point of living if we are not hearing about Krishna? Trees are alive, and they live for a very long time!"

Sūta played the devil's advocate. Gesturing towards the trees that surrounded them in the forest, he said, "Trees are barely alive. They do not even breathe."

"Is breathing the most important part of being alive?" Śaunaka rhetorically asked. "Bellows breath. Should we live like bellows, breathing in and out for years on end?"

"Trees are alive, but they don't breathe." Sūta countered. "Bellows breathe but are not alive. To be alive and breathing is special because then one can enjoy the world."

"What is so special about that?" Śaunaka replied. "Is it special to eat fancy foods? Don't the beasts also feast? It is special to enjoy erotica? Don't beasts also have sex? What is so special about human villagers living like forest beasts? Who would praise and glorify the standard of life enjoyed by dogs, pigs, camels, asses, and so-called humans?

"O Sūta," he passionately continued, "when we don't hear about the heroism of the Hero, the holes of our ears might as well be snake holes. When we do not sing about the One Worth Singing About, we might as well have the tongues of frogs. If the silken crown decorating our head does not bow to the Liberator, it is nothing but a heavy burden! When our hands do not serve Hari, they might as well be the hands of a corpse, uselessly decorated with glittering golden bracelets. Our eyes might as well be the eyes of a peacock feather if they do not look upon the forms of Viṣṇu. Our legs might as well be the roots of trees if we do not walk to Hari's sacred places. We mortals might as well be dead if we never touch the live-giving dust from the feet of blessed devotees! If we do not smell the scent of Tulasī from the beautiful feet of Viṣṇu, what is the use of breathing? We might as well be a breathing corpse."

"Worst of all," Śaunaka concluded, "If we pronounce Hari's name but our heart does not melt and erupt in emotions like tears and goosebumps, then what is the use of our heart? Is it really a heart or is it a chunk of iron?"

Sūta was speechless with delight to hear Śaunaka so boldly declare such strong devotional sentiments.

"My dear boy," Śaunaka pleaded softly, with tears streaming down his face, "please teach us what you learned from that foremost devotee, Vyāsa's son, whose words sooth our minds. He was an expert in self-realization, and the King was asking the very best questions."

Sūta said, "Uttara's son, King Parīkṣit, concentrated his mind ever more deeply and lovingly on Krishna, clearly understanding the spiritual meaning in the answers he heard from Vyāsa's son, Śuka. By that constant, undisturbed meditation he lost even the most deeply rooted possessiveness for anything and everything in his kingdom: his friends, wealth, animals, hometown, children, wife, and even his sense of self.

"His broad mind was completely saturated with interest in hearing about divine love of Krishna. Fully aware of his impending death, he renounced all endeavors for the three ordinary aims of life and very firmly desired heartfelt love for the All-Attractive Son of Vasudeva. So he reacted to Śuka's words in much the same way you have reacted to mine: He wanted to hear more!"[13]

---

[13] Three ordinary aims of life are pleasure, economic security, and social morality *(kāma, artha, dharma).* The final two paragraphs are from the beginning of Chapter Four in the original.

CHAPTER FOUR:

GETTING READY FOR MORE

The king said to Śuka, "Oh pure spiritualist, you understand everything and your words are flawless. By speaking the words of Hari, you've made my darkness disappear. I want to hear more!"

Śuka asked what else he should explain.

The king replied that he would like to understand a topic that even the gods find difficult to comprehend. "How does the All-Attractive use his own powers to create this entire universe?" He asked. "How does he maintain it? And how does he again reduce it to nil? What powers does he employ? In these affairs, what does he personally do, and what does he delegate to others?"

Indeed, the King was extremely eager to hear about Hari. "I have another question about the amazing deeds of All-Attractive Hari," he continued, "which even the learned cannot seem to fathom, in spite of their efforts. The One Being maintains many different forms, and performs deeds through many different incarnations. So, do the principles of matter arise simultaneously from the one being or sequentially from his many expansions?"

Śuka looked at the king with humble eyes that seemed to ask, "Since even the learned cannot fathom such things, why do you think I will be able to answer?"

The king replied, "You are intimate with Godhead, so you understand as much as the All-Attractive himself. In fact, you've fully realized spirituality to the utmost. Therefore I know you can answer my questions."

Śuka Prepares to Reply

By remembering the All-Attractive Master of the Senses, Śuka prepared to give a proper reply to the King's questions and his request for more discussion of Hari's qualities.

The sage folded his hands, lowered his eyes, and said:

"I bow to the many forms of the Supreme Person, which use three powers to enact the eternal pastime of creating, maintaining, and destroying existence. These forms dwell within the being of all embodied beings, although they remain invisible to all angles of vision.

"I bow again to the completely real form of the Supreme Person. He makes unreal sadness disappear, and he destroys real sadness by granting the treasured objectives cherished by the topmost swans of spiritualism.

"Again, again, and yet again I bow to the Supreme Truth who becomes the foremost intimate member of the Yadu dynasty but always remains very distant from empiricists bereft of a heartfelt connection to him. His power and opulence cannot be matched. He enjoys within the spiritual realm of his own abode.

"Celebrating him, remembering him, seeing him, glorifying him, hearing about him, and worshipping him... these clean the stain of misfortune from all people of the world. I bow again and again to he who is so auspicious to hear about.

"The hearts of the wise who strive to worship his feet are freed from all attachments to the here and hereafter, and progress confidently and pleasantly towards the true goal. I bow again and again to he who is so auspicious to hear about.

"Without such dedication to him even the greatest renunciates, donors, sacrificers, thinkers, chanters, and upstanding persons cannot really attain any sure result from their endeavors. I bow again and again to he who is so auspicious to hear about.

"Yet even sinful or uncultured people from any part of the world[14] become pure simply by taking shelter of those who take shelter of him. So I bow again to powerful Viṣṇu.

"He is the soul sought by soul-seekers who study the three Veda, follow morality, and perform austerity. His All-Attractive form is beyond the arguments and logic of even the greatest gods like Brahmā and Śaṅkara. May he be pleased!

"He is the husband of all beauty, all sacrifice, all people, all thoughts, all realms, and all the earth. He personally husbands the paths tread by his devotees. May the All-Attractive Spiritual Husband be pleased with me!

"Philosophers try to describe him as far as their experience allows, but only those whose intellect his been purified by complete concentration upon his feet can truly understand him. May the All-Attractive Enlightener be pleased with me!

"Long ago, he inspired the goddess of intelligence[15] to amplify the faithful memory within Brahmā's heart. Brahmā could then speak properly about the divine. May that sage of all sages be pleased with me!

"That Powerful Person is attracted to dwell within all the things he created from his original substance, and thus enjoys the sixteen qualities expanded from himself.[16] May the All-Attractive create and enjoy the beauty of the words I will speak!

---

[14] "Mountain-tribes, hunter tribes, gypsy-like tribes, farmers, ruffians, Huns, Greeks, Persians and so on."

[15] Transcendental Sarasvatī, an expansion of Śrīmatī Rādhārāṇī.

[16] The sixteen qualities are the five objects of perception (earth, water, fire, air, and ether), five senses of perception (smell, taste, sight, touch, and hearing), five senses of interaction (locomotion, manipulation, consuming, evacuation, and progeneration), and the central coordinator of the senses: the mind.

“Obeisances to the All-Attractive Son of Vasudeva! The affectionate souls who drink the delicate taste emanating from his lotus-like lips become full of knowledge and can create the Veda.”

Chapter Five:

Evolution of the Universe

Śuka looked into Parīkṣit's eyes and said, "My dear King, the questions you've just asked about the origin of the universe are the same questions Nārada asked. Brahmā, the very womb of the Veda, answered them by directly explaining what he had heard from Hari within his heart."

Śuka began to tell the tale of Nārada's conversation with Brahmā:

Nārada approached his father Brahmā and said, "O god of gods, firstborn manifestor of beings, my respects to you. You understand spiritual truths in great detail. Please explain them to me!"

Brahmā replied, "Where should I begin?"

Nārada said, "O capable one, please tell me the factual truths about this world. What is its shape? How is it sustained, created, and destroyed? What is beyond it? And what is it made of?"

Brahmā asked Nārada, "Why do you think I would be able to answer such profound questions?"

Nārada replied, "You certainly know the answers to all these questions, because you are the master of everything that has come into being, everything coming into being, and everything that will come into being. Your comprehension grasps the universe as easily as someone grasps a fruit in their hand."

"You have a very high opinion of me," said Brahmā.

"Yes," Nārada replied, "because you seem to be completely independent, the source of your own knowledge, your own maintainer, and your own refuge."

Brahmā was a bit surprised. He knew such things were not at all true and wondered why that might not be obvious. "What makes you say these things?" he asked.

Nārada replied, "Because you created all beings and all things, on your own, by your own powers, just like a spider effortlessly produces silk. You created all the names, forms, and qualities of everything superior, inferior, and normal. It doesn't seem possible that they could have any remote or direct cause other than your greatness."

Brahmā was quiet, contemplating how to address his son's misconception. An opportunity soon presented itself when Nārada voiced a doubt: "As powerful as you are, you still underwent severe disciplines of meditation, as if you needed to learn something. It appears that you were lacking something and some other source supplied it, so I have a troublesome doubt that you cannot actually be the Supreme Being.

"O master of everything, knower of everything," Nārada continued, "please consider how to answer everything I've asked in a way that my intellect can easily understand."

Is Brahmā the Ultimate Being?

Brahmā was very pleased with his son, and spoke with deep affection. "My loving child," he said, "out of compassion you mercifully ask these fitting questions, which make me joyful because they remind me of the audience I once had with the powers of the All-Attractive. All my powers are a result of that audience.

"The praise you have given me is not entirely false, my son. But it is also not wrong to doubt that I am the Supreme

Being. I can make this universe shine only because that Supreme Being shines. I am like the moon, which shines only because of the light of the sun."

Nārada replied as if he were shocked, "But all over the world people consider you the supreme creator!"

"Bewildered by the insurmountable power of his illusions," Brahmā replied, "selfish people prattle on like this; their wits are dulled by constant obsession with, 'I and mine.' May we respectfully meditate upon the All-Attractive Son of Vasudeva!"

Fools in the grip of illusion dream of themselves as divorced and independent from the Supreme Being. They therefore imagine their heroes, like Brahmā, to be independent and self-made.

What is the Universe Made of?

"The universe," Brahmā said, "has five principles: consciousness, psychology, time, activity, and objects. All five are the supreme spiritual energy of Vasudeva's Son. The fact is that none of them have any true existence separate from him."

Brahmā thus enumerated the five essential principles of existence. The most fundamental principle is consciousness (jīva). Each individual fulcrum of consciousness develops a unique psychological nature (svabhāva) with specific attractions and aversions to various objects (dravya). Time (kāla) facilitates change, thus allowing consciousness to work (karma) towards satisfying its attractions and aversions.

What is Beyond the Universe?

Nārada wanted to know what was beyond the universe. Brahmā answered somewhat cryptically. "The entity beyond the universe is the same entity sustaining it," he said. "Who do you think that might be?"

Nārada answered, "Some sages teach that consciousness, the substance of knowledge itself, sustains the world and is beyond it."

Brahmā did not agree. "Knowledge is not the ultimate entity," he said. "It also has an objective. Ultimately, that objective is Nārāyaṇa."

"Some say the gods sustain the universe," Nārada suggested, "and are beyond it as well."

Brahmā still did not agree. "The gods are merely the limbs of Nārāyaṇa," he said.

"Some say the world is self-sustaining."

"I do not agree," Brahmā said. "The world exists within and is sustained by Nārāyaṇa."

"Some say that sacrifices sustain and support the world," Nārada suggested.

"Not directly," Brahmā said. "Sacrifices aim at satisfying Nārāyaṇa. My boy, all these things have other things beyond them, sustaining them, and towards which they strive. Ultimately they are all sustained by and founded upon Nārāyaṇa.

Nārāyaṇa is the sum and substance...

...of knowledge,

...of the gods,

...of the universe itself,

...of sacrifice,

...of yoga,

...of austerity,

...of philosophy.

"Everything exists within and strives towards Nārāyaṇa," Brahmā concluded. "I create the manifestations he manifests. He resides in the soul of my soul as the all-seeing master, and his glance fills me with creative inspiration."

Evolution of the Universe

Nārada wanted to know how the universe is created, maintained and destroyed.

Brahmā explained: "Essentially, it is all done by nature's three qualities: clarity, passion, and darkness. Clarity maintains the universe, passion creates it, and darkness destroys it."

"Where do these qualities come from?" Nārada asked.

"They are the qualities of that Great Being who is beyond qualification," Brahmā answered.

"How can something 'beyond qualities' possess qualities?" Nārada asked.

"That Great Being," Brahmā explained, "possesses great power. It is actually this power which has qualities."

Earlier, Brahmā had explained that consciousness is the fundamental principle in the universe. Nārada wanted to learn about the relationship between consciousness and these three qualities.

"Consciousness is naturally transcendent to the world," Brahmā explained, "But the three qualities entice consciousness to bind and unify itself with this world."

"How?" Nārada asked. "How do the three qualities so entice consciousness?"

"Consciousness wants to unite with the three qualities because they manifest objects of pleasure and the means for enjoying those objects," Brahmā explained.

"What are those means?" Nārada asked.

"The three qualities offer three powers to consciousness. The first is perception, which acts as the cause of adventure. The second is the object of perception, which is the objective of adventure. The third is the power to act, the adventurous deeds themselves."

"But," Nārada asked, "you described consciousness as 'naturally transcendent to the world.' So how is it possible for consciousness to form a union with the world?"

Brahmā explained that the union is sanctioned and empowered by the all-powerful. "There is an entity beyond the three qualities. That entity is spirit," Brahmā said. "He exists in a realm we cannot perceive. We who are under the grip of those three material qualities cannot see his All-Attractive form. Nonetheless, he is the master of everyone, including me."

Nārada was completely fascinated, and wanted to know the techniques employed by the all-powerful to bind consciousness into a union with the world.

Brahmā explained, "The master of powers uses his power as three tools: time, activity, and psychology. He uses these upon the conscious soul whose freewill is inclined to divorce from the supreme and marry to the world. These three powers form the binding link between consciousness and the objects of the world."

Primordial Evolutions

Nārada wanted to know more details about how the three qualities interact with the five principles to create the world of objects.

Brahmā previously explained that the principle catalyst of evolution is consciousness (jīva). Consciousness develops specific inclinations and desires (svabhāva). The endeavor to fulfill these desires causes evolution to eventually produce the world of objects. Now Brahmā further explained that time (kāla) is the agent of change, so it facilitates evolution in the three qualities (guṇa). Clarity (sattva-guṇa) is the first quality to respond to the combined stimuli of time and desire. It evolves into the primeval universe (mahāt-tattva), which is essentially a blueprint of destined causes and effects (karma).

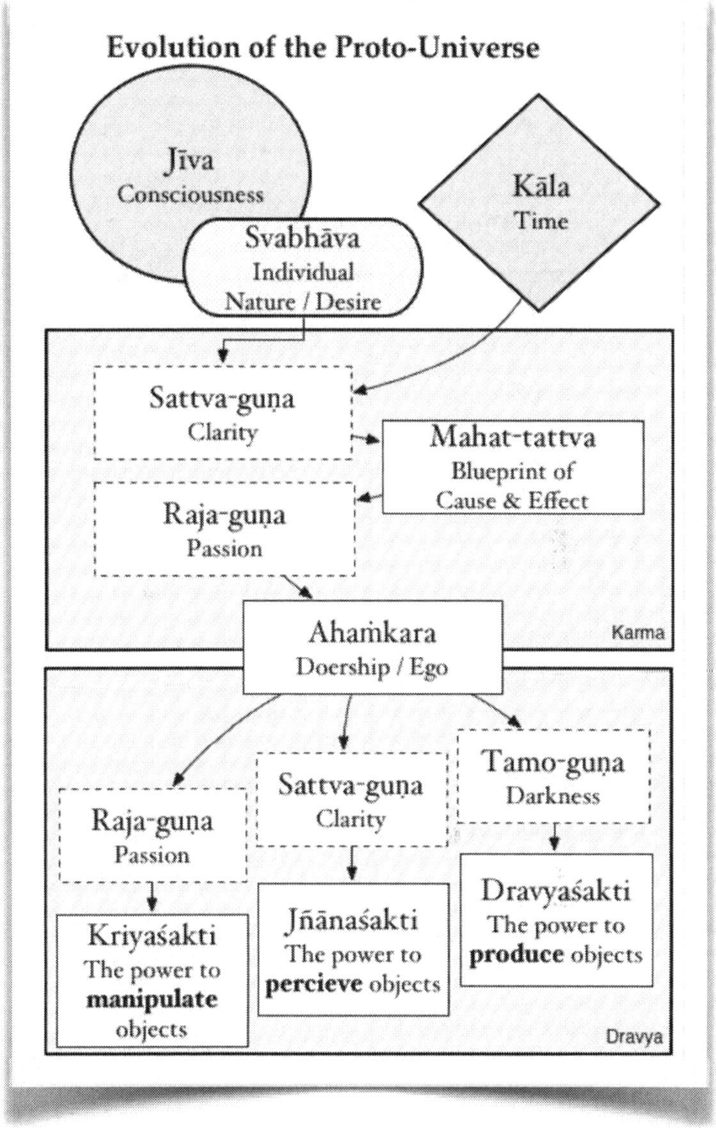

The quality of passion (rajo-guṇa) is the next to respond. It interacts with the primeval universe, causing it to evolve ego (ahaṁkāra). Ego allows consciousness to conceive of itself as an independent, self-initiating doer.

Then, the quality of darkness (tamo-guṇa) interacts with ego to evolves the power to create tangible elements (dravya-śakti). Ego also interacts with the quality of clarity, to evolve the power to perceive tangible things (jñāna-śakti). Ego also interacts with the quality of passion, to evolve the power to manipulate tangible things (kriya-śakti).

Evolution of Tangible Properties

Nārada wanted to know more about each of these three energies that create the tangible universe. First he asked Brahmā to explain how tangible objects evolve from the dravya-śakti.

Brahmā explained that dravya-śakti first produces the element space - the container in which all other objects can exist. Space is tangible by its quantifier, sound.[17]

Space evolves into air, which is tangibly quantified by the sense of touch.[18] Each element also contains the qualities of the evolutionarily previous element; so air also carries sound. Air is special because it supports life by creating power and alertness in body and mind.

"What drives this evolution in the elements?" Nārada asked.

Brahmā answered, "The constant influence of time and destiny, themselves driven by the psychology of the desires held by the living entities who will inhabit the evolving universe."

---

[17] The dimensions of space are revealed ("quantified," made measurable) by the size of the wavelengths that can exist within it. These waves produce sound - large waves are heard as low pitches, small waves as high pitches. The science of spatial acoustics fully exposes the intrinsic relationship between space and sound.

[18] Sound waves in the spatial element generate movement, which creates wind, air, gaseous substance. This movement is key to the sense of touch, which activates when two adjacent surfaces move in relation to one another.

Brahmā continued to explain the evolution of tangible elements: Air evolves into fire, which produces light and is therefore tangible through sight.[19] Fire is also tangible through the previous sensations: its heat can be felt in the sense of touch, and its sound can be heard.

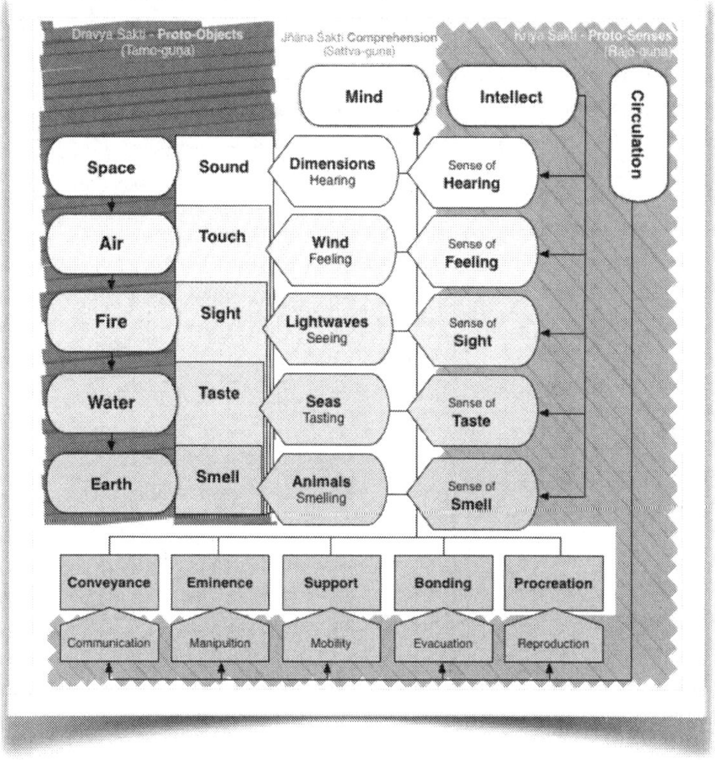

Fire evolves into water, which is tangible by taste.[20] Water is also tangible through the previous sensations: we can see it, feel it, and hear it.

---

[19] Movement in the air causes friction which generates heat and evolves into fire - radiant energy.

[20] Heat generates precipitation, thus water evolves from fire. Water's essence is liquidity, which facilitates mixtures and combinations - the essence of flavor.

Water evolves into earth, tangible through the sense of smell.[21] Earth is tangible through all the previous sensations as well: we can taste, see, feel and hear it.

Evolution of Perception

Nārada then asked Brahmā to explain how jñāna-śakti evolves the ability to perceive and exchange with objects.

"Jñāna-śakti first evolves into a prototype mind," Brahmā said. "Then, the mind's ten divine faculties of perception and interactivity come into being."

"What are these ten divine facilities?" Nārada asked.

Brahmā first enumerated the five divinities of sense perception. "We perceive sound through the divine directions of space (dik)," he said. "We perceive touch through the divinity of wind (vāta); vision, through the divinity of lightwaves (arka); taste, through the alert divinity of the seas (pracetaḥ); and smell, through the divinity of animals (aśvi)."

Next, Brahmā named the five divinities that facilitate exchanges between the senses and their objects. Divine conveyance (vahni) grants the ability to communicate. Divine eminence (indra) grants the ability to manipulate. Divine support (upendra) grants mobility. Divine bonding (mitra) grants the ability to hold and evacuate. Divine procreation (kāḥ) grants the ability to procreate.

Evolution of Sense Organs

Finally, Nārada asked Brahmā to explain how kriya-śakti evolves the biological prototypes of senses, through which these ten divinities can express their powers.

Brahmā explained that kriya-śakti first evolves into a prototype intelligence and prāṇa (vital circulation), each of which then evolve five outlets. Intelligence generates the five senses of perception: hearing, touching, smelling, seeing, and tasting. Prāṇa generates the five senses of action: speech, manipulation, mobility, reproduction, and evacuation.

---

[21] The sediment of the particulate mixtures in liquids evolves into solids, "earth." The sense of smell detects solid particles entering the nose.

Assembling the Primordial Elements

"I've described how the three fundamental qualities of nature interact with the essential material substance, ego," Brahmā said, "and thus generate three powers which produce all the building blocks required for life. Still it is impossible for life to arise in the universe until these individual components somehow come together."

"How does that happen?" Nārada asked.

"Living beings are the energy of the All-Attractive," Brahmā explained. "They are the ultimate catalyst exciting the primordial elements to internetwork with one another and assume successive forms, eventually causing the universe to manifest as we now know it."

"When does all this happen?" Nārada asked.

"It happens during the thousands of uncountable ages while the universe lies submerged in the cosmic ocean. That is when the three qualities interact with ego to evolve the three powers. When this process is finally complete, the Puruṣa and the living entities situated within the forces of time, destiny, and psychology animate the inanimate universe."

Chapter Six:

The Universal Prototype

"You mentioned that the Puruṣa is among the entities who animate the universe. Is he attached to the universe, like the other living entities?" Nārada asked.

"No," Brahmā replied. "He is completely detached and unaffected by the universe."

"Can we still find him within it?" Nārada asked.

"Yes," Brahmā replied. "He has split himself into infinitude, situated nowhere and everywhere with infinite legs, feet, arms, and eyes; infinite mouths and heads."

"How can see his divine presence everywhere?" Nārada asked.

"Those who are wise imagine this universe to be his body," Brahmā replied

"How?" Nārada asked.

"One way," Brahmā said, "is to consider the seven lower realms as the lower part of his body, from the buttocks down, and the seven higher realms as the upper part of his body, from the waist up.

“Another way,” he continued, “is to imagine different types of people to be different organs on the universal body of the All-Attractive. Imagine that intellectuals are his mouth, administrators are his arms, merchants are his legs, and workers are his feet.

Nārada asked Brahmā to expand on the short description he just gave about how the various realms in the universe can be thought of as various parts of the Puruṣa’s body.

Brahmā explained that the seven higher realms (lokas) imaginarily correspond to the seven energy centers, cakras, of Puruṣa:

Satya	Truth	**Forehead**
Tapa	Self-sacrifice	**Face**
Jana	Knowledge	**Neck**
Maha	Saintliness	**Chest**
Sva	Heaven	**Heart**
Bhuva	Sky	**Naval**
Bhū	Earth	**Pelvis**

The seven lower realms (talas) are thought to correspond to seven parts of the lower body:

A	Bottomless	**Buttocks**
Vi	Extreme Depths	**Thighs**
Su	Good Depths	**Knees**
Talā	Below Bottomless	**Shins**
Mahā	Astonishing Depths	**Ankles**
Rasā	Intoxicating Depths	**Feet**
Pā	Feast Depths	**Soles**

"Beyond all this," Brahmā stipulated, "is the eternal spiritual realm."

He explained that some people hold a different, simpler paradigm, in which the earthly realms (bhū) are like his feet, the middle realms (bhuva) his abdomen, and the higher realms (sva) his head.[22]

[22] Here ends Chapter Five in the original Sanskrit.

Universal Form as the Prototype of the Universe

Like King Parīkṣit, Nārada wanted to know how the three fundamental powers are related to the Universal Form of Puruṣa. Brahmā began to explain that all the prototypes generated by the three powers do so as a result of the evolution of the Universal Form. The Universal Form is the essence of all other forms. Everything attains its unique nature as a result of the uniqueness of various features of the Universal Form.[23]

The divinity of communication and the objects of speech, like words and languages, come from his mouth.

The seven types of poetic hymns come from the seven layers of his body.[24]

The flavors of all delicious and nourishing foods, like the feasts offered to the gods and ancestors, come from his tongue.

The divinity of breath and the air come from his nose. Delightful perfumes, medicinal herbs, and the olfactory divinity come from his sense of smell.

The resplendent sun and all the beautiful visual forms it illuminates come from his eyes.

The dimensions of space, and the knowledge-carrying sounds heard thereby come from his ears.

The moving air and the sense of touch, as well as the sacrifices to attain such pleasures, come from his skin. Foliage, especially the trees needed for such sacrifices, come

---

[23] What Brahmā says here is closely parallel to a very important section of Ṛg Veda: 10.90, the *puruṣa sūkta*. Here, Brahmā gives a more elaborate description of what is summarized in *puruṣa śuka* in the line beginning with *sahasra-śīrṣā,* and the three verses starting with *brāhmaṇi 'sya mukham asit* (The Original Person has infinite, omnipresent heads, arms, legs, etc. and is the original source of all the elements of the universe).

[24] Plasma, blood, muscle, fat, bone, marrow, and reproductive fluid.

from the hairs on his body. The clouds come from the hair on his head and face. The hard ore-stones come from his strong nails, and lightning comes from their brilliant polish.

People who protect others come from his arms. Things that grant safety and security, and aid in accomplishing goals, come from Hari's feet. The actions and movements in the world come from his footsteps.

Fertility, semen, fluid, and rain come from his penis. The pleasure of sex comes from his genitals.

The gods of death and of the departed[25] come from his anus - which evacuates and frees the universe from the vile things in its bowels: violence, falsehood, death, torment, and so on. Frustration, immorality, and all sorts of darkness come from his back.

Rivers and streams come from his veins. Mountains come from his bones. The oceans and all nourishment come from his belly, the place all living beings go when the world is destroyed.

The mind comes from his heart. Consciousness, intelligence, morality come from the soul of that Supreme Person, the ultimate origin of everything.

Brahmā concluded by saying, "Me, you, Śiva, the seven first-born sages, the divinities of light, the divinities of darkness, dragons, the paranormals,[26] humanity, birds, beasts, reptiles, serpents, fauna and flora... Everything that exists in the water, on the land or in the sky... Everything that exists, existed, or will exist in this universe... Everything is that Supreme Person. He encompasses everything in this world, yet his origin is just beyond it all."[27]

---

[25] Yama is the god of death. Mitra is the god of bonds, but this makes him the god of relationships, and thus family, and thus the ancestors, and thus the departed spirits.

[26] The "paranormals" are enumerated as: Gandharva, Siddha, Caraṇa, Apsara, Yakṣa, Rakṣa, the hosts of ghosts (Bhūta) and their Pitṛ caretakers.

[27] Here, Brahmā parallels the *puruṣa-sūkta* line, *puruṣa evedaṁ sarvam* (The Original Person is certainly everything in the universe), and, *sa bhūmiṁ*

Divinity Beyond the Universe

Nārada declared, "Amazing! The entity who is the prototype of the universe itself has his roots beyond the universe! This might seem a little difficult to understand, so please illustrate it with an analogy."

"Take life-air (prāṇa) for example," Brahmā suggested. "It energizes the body, but it's energy does not originate in the body, it originates in itself. Another example is the sun. It lends its radiance to all celestial things, like the moon, but shines by its own power. In a similar way, the Supreme Person is situated within his own power, independent of all things, but lends his power to all things. Thus he is both within and beyond everything."

Nārada became very animated, "I really want to know," he pleaded, "how the Supreme Person exists beyond this world. Please explain this to me!"

Brahmā smiled, delighted with his son's spontaneous spiritual inspiration. "My dear boy," he happily said, "The Supreme Person beyond this world is the perfection of fearless nectar, far exceeding any mortal happiness you could possibly imagine! There is no limit to his excellence, but try to understand that the universe we dwell in reflects merely one-fourth of it. His true abode is beyond even what is beyond the three worlds. It is a place of nectar, security, and fearlessness."

"His natural abode is beyond the world that is itself beyond this one?" Nārada asked. "What is the world beyond this one?"

"The world beyond ours," Brahmā said, "represents three-fourths of the Supreme Person. It is the abode of those who are not forced into rebirth. Our three-worlds, on the other hand, are for those subject to rebirth because they have

---

sarvataḥ spṛṣṭvā atyatiṣṭhad daśāṅgulam (He pervades everything in the world, but exists ten widths beyond it).

a selfish bent, being without very strong convictions toward that Supreme Person."[28]

Nārada was sympathetic to the souls who enter rebirth in the selfish world. He asked, "What happens to them?"

"They roam far and wide within these worlds," Brahmā said. "When they are inspired by knowledge they move towards emancipation. When inspired by ignorance they move hungrily towards accumulation. In truth, the Supreme Person is the shelter for both of them."[29]

Nārada wanted to know how the Supreme Person was the shelter of those seeking to accumulate gratification.

Brahmā explained, "Everything ignorant sense gratifiers want to accumulate and enjoy - every sense object, sense organ, and sensual vitality - hatches from the universal egg... which comes from the Supreme Person."

In the ultimate sense, then, both the wise and the ignorant seek the Supreme. Nārada wondered if they were therefore equal. Brahmā explained that the wise are superior because their outlook is more like the divine outlook of the Supreme Person. "The Supreme Person himself," he said, "is uninterested in the material objects he manifests in this world. Such things are like sunshine, but he himself is the brilliant sun!"

A complex question arose in Nārada's mind: "Since everything comes from him, is already his, and is actually him

---

[28] Brahmā parallels many important *puruṣa-sūkta* lines. First, the line *utāmṛtatvasyeśāno uad annenāti-rohati* (He enjoys the greatest nectar, far surpassing mundane pleasures), and the line, *etāvān asya mahimāto jyāyāṁś ca pūruṣaḥ* (The greatness of the original person is extreme). Then the line, *pādo 'sya viśva-bhūtāni tri-pādasy āmṛtaṁ divi* (All living entities exist within this one-fourth. Those in the three-fourths are divine and eternally joyful). Finally, the line, *tripād-ūrdhva udait puruṣaḥ pādo 'syehābhavat punaḥ* (The three-fourths is above and beyond the one-fourth, which is repeatedly manifest and unmanifest).

[29] Here, Brahmā parallels the *puruṣa-sūkta* line, *tato viṣvaṅ vyakrāmat sāśanāśanaśane ubhe* (They wander everywhere, in two directions, towards the real and unreal).

- how can we possibly worship or serve him? What can we possibly offer to the Supreme Person?"

In reply, Brahmā told the story of how he literally faced this situation. "I was born from a lotus flower that sprouted from the belly of that Great Soul," he began. "At that time, I couldn't find anything to use for worship. All I could see were parts of the Original Person.

"To perform a sacrifice for worship," he continued, "many things are required: animals, altars, kuśa grass, a sacred place, a fortuitous time, utensils, herbs, oils, honeys, precious metals, clays, and water. We also need four priests, and three Vedas: Ṛg, Yajur, and Sāma. We have to invoke names, chant mantra, give charity, take oaths, and follow the specific procedures for invoking the gods, commencing, and executing all the details. Finally and certainly, we have to have a clear goal, effective means, ways to atone for mistakes, and the essential offering.

"No such things existed at that time, so I created them from the only entity that did exist - the Universal Form of the Original Person. Then I could perform worship properly. So I worshipped the Original Person with the Original Person.[30]

"From then on," Brahmā continued, "people could use the objects I created from the Original Person to worship the Original person. Your brothers - the nine progenitors - did so, as did many other great souls."[31]

Drawing the discussion to a close, Brahmā summarized, "The foundation of everything that exists is All-Attractive Nārāyaṇa. He is self-sustained beyond everything that exists, while the mighty qualities of his potency create, maintain, and destroy everything. His potency forks into three. One

[30] Here, Brahmā parallels the *puruṣa-sūkta* line, *yajñena yajñam ayajanta* (They utilized Viṣṇu to worship Viṣṇu).
[31] Here, Brahmā parallels the *puruṣa-sūkta* line, *puruṣaṁ jātam agrataḥ tena deva ayajanta* (the gods came in front of the Original Person and worshipped him). "Other great souls" refers to the Manus (human forefathers), sages, ancestors, scholars, religious people, and all people in general.

allows Brahmā to create. Another empowers Hara[32] to destroy. The third allows the Puruṣa himself to maintain everything.

LIMITS OF THE UNLIMITED

Brahmā paused and smiled towards his son in satisfaction. "My dear boy," he said, "I have explained everything you've asked about. The essence of all my answers is that nothing real or unreal exists except the All-Attractive.[33] Never think otherwise."

Nārada said, "I understand, but people might become confused about this when many different sages and scientists give so many different descriptions of reality."

"Yes," Brahmā said plainly, "but I am Brahmā. There is not a speck of falsehood in what I've spoken. Unlike other people my mind never misconceives, nor do my senses ever misperceive."

Nārada asked, "Why are your mind and senses so uniquely clear?"

"Because Hari himself dwells within and clarifies my heart," Brahmā answered.

"Is he not in everyone's heart as the Supersoul?" Nārada asked.

"I am not speaking of the Supersoul - the completely dispassionate, silent observer and permitter within everyone's heart. I speak of Hari himself. He personally clarifies my heart because I very passionately adore him."

"How did this happen?" Nārada asked. "How did you develop such an intimate relationship with Hari?"

---

[32] Śiva

[33] "Real" refers to permanent phenomena beyond the illusory universe. "Unreal" refers to temporary phenomena within the illusory realm. Everything from both spheres is an extension of the All-Attractive.

"I made extreme endeavor," Brahmā replied. "I practiced yoga with great care and expertise, and I attained its success in perfect trance."

"Do you perfectly understand Hari?" Nārada probed.

"Who can perfectly understand him?" Brahmā exclaimed. "Despite my efforts, my unique qualification as the original being and the source of all other sources in this universe, and despite the exalted goal I achieved, I still cannot perfectly understand Hari. That is the nature of Hari. Even he does not perfectly understand himself!"

"But the he is omniscient," Nārada inquired, "How can he not fully know himself?"

"Because he is unlimited!" Brahmā said.

"he is unlimited, but he cannot fully know himself?" Nārada puzzled. "It seems like a contradiction."

"Space is an unlimited substance," Brahmā suggested. "All other substances exist within it. Does space contain its own limit? If so, how is it unlimited? Must we say space is not unlimited because it does not contain its own limit?"

Nārada understood Brahma's point. It is meaningless to say that something which cannot reach its own limit is not unlimited. The nature of "unlimited" is to "lack" a limit. Hari lacks limitation - that is the very nature of being unlimited. A lack of limitation is not a "lack" in the common sense. The inability to exhaustively comprehend an unlimited topic is therefore not a flaw in comprehension, it is the very nature of the comprehension. Perfection is a dynamic thing.

Here logic begins to fear that it will melt. But if we approach the topic humbly, respectfully, and carefully - the logic of it will shine with an unparalleled molten brightness and clarity. Therefore Brahmā recommended, "Let us offer adoration unto his feet, which cut material existence off from his devotees and usher them into all joy and auspiciousness. His extraordinary nature easily bewilders the logical intellect - which is mainly suited for understanding the world it is a part of. By logic alone no one can really understand the true nature of the Supreme Being - not me; not any of you who come after me; not the destroyer; and certainly not lesser beings like the gods."

"Then what should we do," Nārada inquired. "How can we come to know him?"

"Even though people like us cannot fully comprehend him," Brahmā replied, "we can comprehend enough to offer him our respect."

"What is the best way to do so?" Nārada asked.

"The best way to offer respect to the All-Attractive," Brahmā explained, "is to sing about the deeds he does in his incarnations (avatāra)."

Nārada understood. By singing about the All-Attractive we develop pure affection for him. It is this infinite love, not finite intellect, which allows us to truly comprehend the Supreme Being.

Chapter Seven:

Avatāra

Nārada voiced a doubt, "Some say that these incarnations are limited material projections of the truly unlimited Supreme Being."

Brahmā did not agree. He firmly declared that the avatāra are identical to the original, unborn Supreme Being himself; and this applies even those avatāra who only exist in relation to this world - repeatedly creating, maintaining, and destroying it. There is nothing extraneous, projected or conditioned about any incarnation or manifestation of the Supreme. His self is always purely within himself, created by himself and composed purely of himself.

"His manifest forms," Brahmā explained, "are identical to his essential self. They are forms of pure, unmitigated cognition, distinct from other entities yet also one with them all. They are beginningless and endless, eternally and entirely real, beyond subjective qualification, and without any a duality between the body and the embodied."

"This bends the limits of thought," Nārada said.

"Yes," Brahmā replied, "but exalted philosophers like you can comprehend it if you fully purify your heart, mind and senses. Trying to figure out the infinite by logic and argument alone will distort everything and the true concept will vanish."

The Avatāra of Outer Energies

"Please say more about the avatāra who exist only for the sake of this material world," Nārada requested.

"The Original Person, Puruṣa, is the first of such avatāra," Brahmā explained, "Everything we just discussed about the primal creation - time, nature, cause & effect, mind, physical elements, the ego, the three qualities, the senses, everything that proceeds and everything that is original, everything that moves and everything that does not - all of these are merely fragmental expansions of him.

"Every archetype in the creation is him," Brahmā said. "This includes me, Śiva, and Viṣṇu; the Prajāpatis headed by Dakṣa; you and your good brothers; the lords of heaven, lords of the sky, lords of the Earth, and lords of the nether; the masters among the celestial artists; the masters among the demons, monsters, serpents and dragons; the chiefs of sages, ancestors, perfectionists, and of hedonists and rebels, too. It includes monsters like zombies, witches, ghosts, and evil spirits. It includes animals, too - the greatest animals in the sky, on the land, or in the water. Everything extraordinarily attractive, great, potent, powerful, merciful, beautiful, humble, opulent, intelligent and wondrous is nothing but him.

"But this is misleading," Brahmā admitted. "It is more accurate to say that all such beings appear to be portions of the Puruṣa, but in fact are merely portions of his outer energies, not his true inherent nature."

The Avatāra of Inner Energies

"Please," Nārada requested, "tell me now about the avatāra who embody the true inherent nature of the Supreme Person."

"Yes, O sage," Brahmā agreed. "That should be our main topic of discussion. Avatāra who display the true inherent nature of the All-Attractive are known as the līlā-avatāra. I'll introduce them briefly, one after another. Everything foul will evaporate from whoever drinks these delightful descriptions through their ears."

Brahmā described that the Supreme Being, the summum bonum, displays unlimited forms. He began by mentioning Varāha, the boar: "He took this form to enter the great ocean and lift up the world. When the original demon arrived there, he pierced the fiend with his tusk - just like the lightning splits a mountain."[34]

Next, Brahmā mentioned the avatāra who took the post of Indra when no one else could: "Suyajña, the son of Ākūti and Ruci, and his wife Dakṣiṇā gave birth to the immortals known as Suyamā. Because he stole the great fear of the three worlds, Svāyambhuva Manu named him 'Hari.'"

Brahmā continued to enumerate the primary avatāra: "He incarnated as Kapila in the house of Kardama, from the womb of Devahūti, accompanied by nine sisters. He taught his mother about self-realization, revealing the method to wash off the mud of material nature that soils the soul.

"He became known by the name Atri's Gift (Dattātreya) because he answered Atri's prayers for a child. He said, 'I am so satisfied with you that I will give you myself as your child.' The pollen from the lotus of his feet purified the existence of kings like Yadu and Haihaya, granting them spiritual and material fortune."

Brahmā then spoke of the All-Attractive's avatāra among his own children - the quadruplets, Sanaka, Sanat, Sanandanana, and Sanātana: "In the very beginning, I underwent austerity to create the multifaceted universe. As a result, the Eternal One became the Four Sanas. They perfectly explained the spiritual knowledge that had been lost during the destructive flood at the end of the previous cycle of

[34] Chapter Seven in the Sanskrit begins here.

creation. Because of their effort, sages can now clearly comprehend spirituality.

"To illustrate the power of celibacy he incarnated as Nārāyaṇa and Nara," Brahmā continued, "children of Mūrti, the daughter of Dakṣa and wife of Dharma. The armies of Eros tried to destroy their vows, but when they saw themselves and many other divine beauties emanating from All-Attractive Nara-Nārāyaṇa they realized they could never win. Eros had been defeated before, but never like this - without effort or anger. Śiva had once destroyed lust by glancing wrathfully at it. Although wrath can destroy lust, wrath itself remains wild and out of control. Nara-Nārāyaṇa were untouched by wrath. Wrath is terrified to enter within the All-Attractive, so how can lust ever hope to find a place within his mind?"

Brahmā then spoke of **Pṛśnigarbha**:

"Pierced by the sharp words of his stepmother, a small boy left his father's kingdom to practice austerities in the forest. The 'Refuge of Dhruva' granted the boys desires by giving him a reward that sages glorify from every angle."

Brahmā then mentioned **Pṛthu**:

"When Vena strayed from the moral path, curses from the learned fell upon him like lightning bolts - destroying his power and fortune, and casting him down. Fulfilling everyone's needs, the All-Attractive then became Vena's son, saved his father, and saved the world by 'milking' the land for all kinds of crops."

Brahmā then described **Ṛṣabha**-deva:

"Incarnating as the son of Nābhi and Sudevī, he became the best of all humans. He attained equal vision by practicing the yoga of absolute apathy. Great souls try to follow his path and also become the topmost swans of humanity - self-reposed, with pacified senses and completely free of all involvement with the world."

Then, he described **Hayagrīva**:

"Once, when I desired to perform a ceremony, the All-Attractive object of all ceremonies, appeared right in front of me with the head of a horse and an extremely brilliant complexion. He breathed through his nose and the vibration created the beautiful hymns used for ceremonies, the mantras that grant knowledge, and the prayers to all the gods."

He then described **Matsya:**

"When the age came to an end I became very afraid because all the Vedic paths I had spoken of were in danger of being forgotten in the fearsome floods. Manu then saw the All-Attractive incarnate as a fish to protect all the living beings of the world as he enjoyed those dangerous waters."

Next, he described **Kurma.**

"While the leaders of gods and demons were both trying to get the nectar of immortality by churning the sea of milk, the Original Divinity assumed the form of a tortoise. He held the churning-mountain on his shell and its rotation destroyed his itch, allowing him to enjoy a good nap."

Then, Brahmā described **Nṛsiṁha**:

"He who removes the greatest fears of the three world took the form of a man-lion, with frowning eyebrows and a mouth of fearsome teeth. The king of demons swiftly attacked him with a mace, but the man-lion's nails soon shredded the demon-king who writhed on his lap."

Brahmā described the incarnation known as **Hari**:

"When a superior foe dragged the lord of elephants by the leg into the river, the pain-stricken elephant held up a lotus flower and called out, 'Original Person! Master of All! Supreme Topic! Your name brings all good fortune!' Inconceivable Hari heard this sincere plea for shelter, took his cakra weapon and came on the wings of the king of birds. Out of compassion, the All-Attractive destroyed the crocodile's mouth and, with his own hand, rescued the elephant."

Brahmā then described **Vāmana**:

"Although the eldest of all, the Lord of Sacrifice became the youngest son of Aditi (the mother of the gods) and stepped beyond the limits of this world. That small boy claimed the whole world by begging just three deceptive steps from Bali. This was deceptive, but it was plainly begged for and willingly granted, and thus did not transgresses the moral path.

"As for Bali," Brahmā continued, "He did not care for the property he had conquered from the gods. Instead he eagerly took as his crown the water that washed the feet of this avatāra, whose steps are most amazing. He did not desire anything except to fulfill his promise. My dear boy, he even gave himself to fulfill that promise, because his mind was exclusively dedicated to Hari."

Brahmā then spoke of the avatāra who appeared to Nārada, the swan, **Haṁsa**:

"Completely satisfied by your extremely intense affection, the All-Attractive incarnated to speak to you. He taught you how to understand mysticism and philosophy in the excellent, fully illuminated and detailed manner that reveals pure devotion to Vasudeva's Son."

Then, Brahmā described the fourteen **manvantara**-avatāra: "Within each subcycle of creation he appears in Manu's dynasty. His power, like that of his cakra, is unconquerable from any angle. With it, he maintains the world and subjugates vile leaders. His famous deeds are gloriously established in all the three words and beyond."

Brahmā described **Dhanvantari**: "The All-Attractive, who is certainly fame itself, became the avatāra named Dhanvantari. Using his portion of the reclaimed nectar he quickly removed disease from ever-ill humans, by teaching the science of medicine."

Brahmā then described **Paraśurāma**: "When the hell-bent government strayed from the moral path by controverting the spirit of the law described philosophers, the Great Soul turned them into oil in a sacrifice to their own fate. With his very sharp, horribly powerful axe, he uprooted those thorns from the earth, thrice seven times over."

The Rāma Avatāra

Brahmā then began to describe a very special avatāra, Rāma: "Mercifully smiling upon all of us," he said, "the gentle lord descended with his expansions into the dynasty of Ikṣvāku. Ordered by his parents, he dwelt in the forest with his wife and brothers. He foiled and destroyed a ten-headed foe!

"When his eyes smoldered like those of the god of destruction about to burn the world to ashes, the trembling ocean fearfully and quickly granted him a path to his enemy's city."

Nārada asked, "Why was he so enraged?"

Brahmā explained, "His glance burned red-hot in wrath over the grief caused to his kidnapped sweetheart."

"The ocean is a huge mass of cool water," Nārada said. "Why was it afraid of those burning eyes?"

Brahmā replied, "All the ocean's creatures - even the huge crocodiles, sea-serpents, and capricorns - were burning in the heat radiating from his glance!"

"How powerful was Rāma's ten-headed foe?" Nārada asked.

Brahmā explained, "His name was Rāvaṇa, The Ravenous Bringer of Wailing. The great Indra once tried to attack Rāvaṇa by charging with his elephant, but when the elephant's tusk struck Rāvaṇa's breast it shattered, sending white dust everywhere while Rāvaṇa laughed."

"Did he laugh when Rāma attacked?" Nārada asked.

"The wife-stealer's laughter was cut short," Brahmā said, "when he heard Rāma's resounding bow rushing towards him from amidst the soldiers."

The Krishna Avatāra

Brahmā then described the most important avatāra, Krishna: "The brilliantly-black Master of Pleasure, Krishna," he said, "will descend to erase the Earth's pain."

"What pain?" Nārada asked.

"The pain she suffers," Brahmā replied, "from bearing the burden of hordes of vile schemes and schemers." It seems Brahmā referred to the hordes of armies amassed by vile, selfish politicians, but more to the point he referred to the ever-proliferating vile schemes of selfishness that burden every earthling's heart. The Krishna avatāra descends especially to remove this burden from the Earth.

"How will Krishna remove this burden?" Nārada asked.

"His extraordinarily uncommon ways will demonstrate the unsurpassable greatness of his being," Brahmā said. It seems he referred to Krishna's extraordinary display of power in destroying the armies of greedy kings, but in truth he spoke more directly about how Krishna would display his incalculably sweet and attractive intimate pastimes to free our hearts from the burdensome armies of self-centered schemes. Sweetness and beauty is the true measure of Krishna's unsurpassable greatness.

Perceiving the parallel meanings in Brahmā's words, Nārada asked, "How does Krishna destroy demons yet display sweetness at the same time?"

"As a sweet little infant," Brahmā explained, "he will take the life of a huge demon. While just three months old, he will kick over a strong cart and uproot two huge trees just by crawling in between them.[35] It's impossible for anyone else, even the other avatāra, to do such things."[36]

---

[35] Arjuna trees(Terminalia Arjuna) are notoriously tall (20-25 meters) and have extremely strong trunks and roots.

[36] Vāmana was a small boy who defeated a great demon - but he had to transform into a huge, awesome form to do so. Nṛsiṁha kicked over huge pillars, similar to how Krishna uprooted the trees, but Nṛsiṁha required

"Please give more examples of the simultaneous power and sweetness in Krishna!" Nārada enthusiastically requested.

"When Vraja's animals and their protectors die from drinking poisonous water," Brahmā said, "he will bring them back to life simply by showering them with his loving glances. Then he will rigorously punish the mystical serpent whose flickering tongue spits the most viciously powerful poisons, just so he can enjoy playing in the purified pools with his friends.

"That very night," Brahmā continued, "when all of Vraja is sleeping, a blazing fire will sweep through the dry woods of the forest, carrying their certain doom. But Krishna and his brother Balarāma tell everyone to close their eyes and miraculously save them all by godlike, incomprehensible prowess."

"What would happen to their sweet, intimate and confidential affection," Nārada asked, "If the residents of Vraja opened their eyes and saw the awe-inspiring divine majesty of Krishna?"

Brahmā explained that this happens all the time. He gave an example. "Wanting to punish her son, the cowherd woman who is his mother will reach here and there for more rope, but all the rope from the entire village will prove insufficient to bind him. Then, he will open his mouth to show her that no amount of rope can bind him because all of existence is within him. His mother will study the vision carefully with confused thoughts, but soon return to her affectionate business of disciplining her naughty boy."

Nārada was thrilled to hear how the pure, innocent love of Krishna prevails over his power and majesty. "Please give more examples!" He asked.

Brahmā explained that Krishna clearly demonstrates his superiority to the gods and his divine position as the master

---

powerful, fearsome feet to do so. Varāha also uprooted something enormous, the Earth, but to do so he had to become an enormous boar with powerful tusks.

of Vaikuṇṭha, the spiritual world - yet the sweet and intimate love of Vraja never diminishes or becomes awestruck.

"He will defeat Varuṇa," Brahmā said, "by freeing his father Nanda from the god's fearful noose. He will defeat the son of Maya by rescuing the cowherd boys from the caves the demon locked them in. When all of Gokula lay down at night, so exhausted from working hard throughout the day, he will show them that they all dwell with him in Vaikuṇṭha."

"When he becomes seven years old he will deprive a god of the cowherder's sacrifice," Brahmā enthusiastically continued. "That god will send torrential downpours to flood Vraja, but Krishna will compassionately protect Vraja's creatures by holding a mountain aloft as if it were an umbrella, playfully and effortlessly in one hand for seven straight days."

Unable to stop, Brahmā continued to describe how Krishna's all-powerful sweetness drowns out the obvious perception of his all-powerful majesty. "When he turns his attention to enjoying the Rāsa Dance," Brahmā said, "his swooning artistic melodies will ignite the fires of lust among the wives of Vraja's men, as the moonlight illuminates the nighttime forest. When a minion of the wealth-god tries to steal those women, Krishna will steal his head."

Nārada wondered, "What happens to these villains when Krishna does away with them?"

Brahmā explained, "Pralamba the impersonator, Dhenuka the ass, Baka the quack, Keśi the horse, Ariṣṭha the bull; all the wrestlers and all the kings;[37] all the battlefields full of powerful, armed warriors...[38] All of them will be killed by Hari or through his instruments like Balarāma, Arjuna and Bhīma. All of them will attain Hari's own abode, Vaikuṇṭha, or at least the invisible platform of spirituality."

---

[37] Kings specifically mentioned: Kaṁsa, Kālayavana, Dvivida, Pauṇḍraka, Śālva, Naraka, Balvala, Saptokṣa, Śambara, Vidūratha, and Rukmī's clan.

[38] Armies specifically mentioned hail from: Kāmboja, Matsya, Kuru, Sṛñjaya, Kekaya and so on.

Later Avatāra

Nārada asked, "What avatāras become active after Krishna?"

Brahmā mentioned **Vyāsa:**

"As time wears on, humanity will become short-lived and closed minded, and spiritual knowledge will move far beyond their grasp. Sympathetic to this, he cyclically appears from the womb of Satyavatī to divide the tree of the Veda into branches that are relevant to contemporary people."

Brahmā then mentioned Buddha, who enchants the technologically advanced but morally deprived by spreading a philosophy of simple concepts, like non-violence:

"Eventually, the god's enemies will use mysterious, swift, and invisible fortresses to destroy people who are devoted to righteous ways. He will then empower an avatāra to enchant their minds by many gorgeous glorifications of somewhat moral principles."

Brahmā concluded by describing Kalki:

"When there is no discussion of Hari even in the homes of 'saints;' when twice-born, lowborn, and rulers are all animals; when not even a word can be heard anywhere about mantras, ceremonies, or altars; then, at the end of the Kali-age, the All-Attractive will become the chastiser."

Incarnations within Material Nature

Brahmā had summarized the līlā-avatāra, the incarnations of the All-Attractive who exhibit a glimpse of his active nature. Now Nārada asked to about the guṇa-avatāra, beings who exemplify the powerful qualities of the All-Attractive.

In reply, Brahmā explained that the power of the All-Attractive expresses itself in the material world in three modes: the creative mode - passion, the sustaining mode - clarity, and the destructive mode - darkness. Each mode has an avatāra in charge of it. Brahmā himself is the avatāra for the creative mode of passion. Viṣṇu is the avatāra for the sustaining mode of clarity. Śiva is the avatāra for the destructive mode of darkness.

Each mode also has a quality which represents it. Struggle is the avatāra of creative passion. Integrity is the avatāra of sustaining clarity. Disintegrity is the avatāra of destructive darkness.[39]

Each mode also has beings who represent it. Those who generate ideas and substances, like the seven sages and nine progenitors, are avatāra of creative passion. Providers of sustenance and government, like the immortals and the Manu, are avatāra of sustaining clarity. Beings driven by anger, like the anti-gods, are avatāra of destructive darkness.

	Clarity	**Passion**	**Darkness**
Controllers	Viṣṇu	Brahmā	Śiva
Powers	Integrity	Struggle	Disintegrity
Exemplars	Sustainers: gods and human leaders	Creators: progenitors, inventors	Destroyers: anti-gods and angry beings

Brahmā clarified that guṇa-avatāra are not on the same level as līlā-avatāra. Although they do represent a portion of the All-Powerful, still their greatness is confined within this illusory realm.

"Viṣṇu is far greater than the limits of this illusory realm," Brahmā continued to explain. "Even a scientist who could count all the particles of dust on earth would not be able to count all the glories of Viṣṇu. His swift and firm step surpassed the roof of the universe and agitated the unagitated energetic equilibrium. Not even I can find the limit of the Mystically Powerful Personality, nor can the sages born before you, what to speak of those who are junior to us!

---

[39] *Tapa* - Struggle; *Dharma* - integrity; *Adharma* - disintegrity.

The origin of divinity in this world, Śeṣa, sings of the qualities of the All-Attractive with ten hundred mouths and even to this day has not found their limit!"

Definite Perception of the Infinite

Since Viṣṇu is unlimited, Nārada wondered how it could be logically possible for him to directly appear within the definite, defined names and forms of the līlā-avatāra.

Brahmā explained, "The mercy of the All-Attractive is also infinite! He bestows it to those who, without pretense, fully give their entire being to him. As a result, these fortunate souls cross beyond the insurmountable divine mysteries. Others, whose thoughts of 'I and mine' remain limited to a corpse that will be eaten by dogs and jackals can never comprehend the unlimited avatāra."

"Can you give examples of people who have received this mercy," Nārada asked, "and can thus comprehend the All-Attractive avatāra to a significant extent?"

"My dear son," Brahmā replied, "here are the foremost of those who have attained this mysterious mercy of the Supreme: myself, yourself, and blessed Śiva; Prahlāda, the best of the demons; Svāyambhuva Manu and his wife and their children; Prācīnabarhi, Ṛbhu, and even Aṅga; Dhruva, Ikṣvāku, Aila, Mucukunda, Videha, Gādhi, Raghu, Ambarīṣa, Sagara; Gaya, Nāhuṣa and the rest; Māndhātā, Alarka, Śatadhanu, Anu, Rantideva, Bhiṣma of godly oath, Bali, Amūrttaraya, Dilīpa; Saubhari, Utaṅka, Śibi, Devala, Pippalāda, Sārasvata, Uddhava, Parāśara, Bhūriṣeṇa; and others like Vibhīṣaṇa, Hanumān, Śuka, Arjuna, Arṣṭiṣeṇa, Vidura, and Śrutadeva."

"These are all very unusual persons," Nārada asked. "Is it possible for more common people to comprehend the infinite All-Attractive?"

"Yes," Brahmā answered. "Common people like housewives and laborers, and even animals and uncivilized humans can also receive the infinite mercy of the All-Attractive and thus surmount the insurmountable divine mysteries."

Nārada was amazed and inspired. "How?" he asked.

"Although they don't have a pure background," Brahmā said, "they can attain this incomparable status if they learn how to cultivate devotion to the Amazing Actor."

"How would they learn that?" Nārada asked.

"By deeply hearing about him," Brahmā replied.

"When they surmount the insurmountable mysteries," Nārada asked, "What do they realize?"

"Some realize Paramātmā, the 'Supersoul'," Brahmā said. "He is eternally extremely placid, fearless, and the substance of all cognizance. He is uncontaminated by and absolutely equal towards all causes and effects."

"What about others," Nārada asked, "what do they realize?"

"Others may realize Brahman," Brahmā said.

"Can you describe Brahman?" Nārada asked.

"No, not exactly," Brahmā admitted. "They experience it as a type of happiness arising from the lack of all grief. Brahman is beyond words, because words always have dualities and objectives."

"And others?" Nārada probed still further. "What do they realize when they are graced to cross beyond the insurmountable mysteries?"

Brahmā replied, "Some others may realize Bhagavān - the All-Attractive Supreme Person, of whom Paramātmā and Brahman are parts, and in front of whom illusion flees bashfully."

"Is there any further realization?" Nārada inquired.

"No," Brahmā replied. "Those who realize the infinite as All-Attractive Bhagavān become self-illuminating. They have no further need for meditations, restrictions, regulations, rituals, and so on; just as the rain-god has no need to dig a well.

"Bhagavān is all-encompassing and all-attractive," Brahmā continued. "He is everything desirable! From him flows the complete perfection of every endeavor that our acquired or inherent natures may aspire for. Even when everything is destroyed, even when the body collapses and crumbles into its elements, still the eternal accomplishment of realizing Bhagavān is never vanquished - just like the sky always remains intact, no matter how bad the storm."

"Dear boy," Brahmā concluded, "All-Attractive Bhagavān is the one I have spoken about as the manifestor of everything. Without him, no other cause or effect can exist."

Elaborate On This

Brahmā looked upon his son very affectionately. "The All-Attractive himself enlightened me on all these topics," he said. "I have explained them to you as, 'The Beautiful Tales of the All-Attractive.' Now you please elaborate upon this compilation of his glories. Expand it so that devotion for All-Attractive Hari - the soul of all and the repose of all - can flourish among humanity."

Nārada was honored and inspired. "Should I elaborate on those portions that have to do with the material world," he asked. "Or should I only focus on the All-Attractive in his own spiritual context?"

"You should elaborate on both," Brahmā replied, "including how to appreciate the material world as an emanation from the Supreme Master. Those who regularly and attentively hear such things are never bewildered by materialism."

Chapter Eight: Parīkṣit's Questions

The story had come to a close, but the King's hunger to hear was not satiated. He addressed Śuka with great feeling, "How did Nārada expand upon what he learned from Brahmā? To whom did he speak and what did he say? Certainly it would be amazing, because Nārada had personal audience with the divine and was personally directed by Brahmā to narrate the qualities of He Who Is Beyond Qualifications. You are foremost among those who understand reality," the King continued, "I want to understand reality from you. Please speak to me about Hari, whose heroism is astounding and whose conversation is the most auspicious thing in all the world."

Śuka might want to test the King, "You want to keep hearing me speak about Hari? Have you no other concerns? After all, you are on the verge of death."

So the King said, "I am already prepared to cast aside this body. My mind has already relinquished its attachments. Its only desire is to enwrap itself within Krishna - the true soul of everyone and everything. Please converse with me about him, so that I may become as greatly fortunate as you are."

Śuka might further test him, "Why do you want to enwrap your mind in Krishna during your final moments?"

So the King said, "All-Attractive Krishna is like a bee who soon appears in the lotus-flower-soul of a person who always, seriously, and confidentially strives to hear about him. He enters the heart through the hallways of the ears and cleanses all impurity from its lake of emotions, just as autumn makes the lakes clear. With a pure heart, one who hears about Krishna soon becomes a swan who never disentangles from his embrace on the lotus-root, Krishna's feet. Liberated from all causes of suffering, he feels like a traveler finally returned to his own sweet home."

Śuka was very happy to hear King Parīkṣit express so much affection for hearing about Krishna. "I will tell you the many ways Nārada expanded these Beautiful Tales," he said. "But first, do you have any questions about what I've already said?"

Questions About Bodies and Souls

Indeed the King was an unparalleled listener, and so had dozens of questions. "Since the soul is unrelated to inert material elements," he asked, "why does it root into a body made of such elements? Is this intentional, or is there some other cause? I am asking you because I trust that you really understand the answer.

"I also have a question about Puruṣa's body," the king continued, "from whose navel grows a unique lotus in which all the worlds exist. Besides its gigantic size, how is it different from the body of an ordinary soul?

"I also have a question about Brahmā's body. He was born from that beautiful naval-lotus, so he is like the Puruṣa's child. A child grows into a specific type of adult because of the parent's affection; similarly Brahmā became what he is, the creator of the bodies of all creatures, as a result of the Puruṣa's affection. Since he seems to be the offspring of the Puruṣa, how is his body different from the Puruṣa's body?"

The king also wanted to know where the Puruṣa could be found. "The Puruṣa lies in a place that allows him to be in touch with everything, yet be touched by nothing - he can affect the sustenance, manifestation, and dissolution of everything yet remain completely unbound by all of it, as the self-powered master of all powers. Lying in that one place he can simultaneously lie within the hearts of all beings. Where is this mysterious place?"

The king had a question about the universal form. "Is the Puruṣa's body made from the world, or is the world made from the Puruṣa's body?"

Questions About The Universe

The king wanted to know about a fundamental ingredient of the universe, time. "How is time measured?" he asked. "What do the words 'past, future, and present' really mean? What are the lifespans of various beings? What are the major and minor cycles of universal time? Where does time begin? Why is it perceived in both minute and gigantic ways? How is it related to activity? There are many theories about such things, but I want to know your opinion, because you are the most spiritual scholar."

The king had questions about units of time called ages. "What are the potencies and durations of the universal ages?" he asked. "What religions are specific to each age? What amazing deeds are performed in each age by the avatāra of Hari?"[40]

Another fundamental ingredient of the universe is the principle of cause-and-effect. The king also had several questions about this. "Activities are causes, how do they produce effects?" he asked. "Which activities are the causes of which effects? How does a soul invested into the qualities of matter get the power to perform actions within the inert world, thus generating effects that fulfill its desires?"

---

[40] This paragraph comes two paragraphs later in the original Sanskrit.

The king also had questions about the physical dimensions and composition of the universe. "The earth, the nether regions, the four corners of the sky, the planets, stars, mountains, rivers, seas, and islands..." he asked, "How did they become what they are? Who inhabits them? What are the dimensions of this fertile egg in which we exist? What are its micro- and macro-cosmic units?"

The king had questions about the living beings who inhabit the universe. "What are the deeds of great beings?" he asked. "What is the social system that facilitates both their practical and spiritual progress? What moral duties are common to all humans, and which ones are unique to certain individuals? Especially, what are the moral duties of kings who wish to qualify as spiritualists; and what are the moral duties of living beings that are in distress?"

His questions began to turn toward transcendence, as he began to inquire directly about spiritual paths. "Please enumerate the fundamental elements and explain how their inherent and subsidiary qualities can be properly used to worship the Puruṣa. What is the yogic path of self-realization? What masteries come to those who masters it? How do they curb their unreal self? What paths are defined in the Veda, it's appendices, the histories, and the Purāṇas?"

Now the king began to ask about liberation and devastation. "How have all creatures wandered into this devastating world?" he inquired. "How will they escape it? While they are here, what is the proper way to satisfy the divinities and fulfill their desires for pleasure security, and cooperation? After the destruction of this world, fettered souls are laid into deep sleep. How do they become manifest again during the next creation? What is the self - in a bound state, in a liberated state, and situated in its own intrinsic form?"

Finally, the king inquired about the supreme topic, the All-Attractive."Please explain how the All-Attractive is supremely independent yet depends on his own potencies for enjoyment, all while remaining detached from such potencies, as the great, neutral observer. Please answer all my questions in direct relation to the All-Attractive."

Everyone was deeply inspired and impressed by the profundity and sophistication of the kings questions. Worried that Śuka would feel shy to answer all these question, or might not think the king qualified to understand the answers, he said, "I hope to understand your answers because I have deep trust in your knowledge. I fully submit myself to you, great sage. In all these subjects, you are as authoritative as the supreme, self-born divinity. Others merely repeat what they have learned from those who have come before them, but you have the deepest comprehension of all because you personally understand the answers you give.

"O spiritualist," the king concluded, "I may be fasting, but I am not tired at all because I am drinking the elixir of Infallible Nectar flowing like a river from the ocean of your words."

In fact Śuka was thrilled by the kings intricate, exacting and eager questions about Krishna, the Protector of the Saintly. His affection for the king deepened. He humbly appreciated that he was protected by his spiritual realization, but the king, as a child, had been personally protected by Viṣṇu himself. Śuka was also glad that the audience would benefit from hearing their discussion. He recommenced narrating the Purāṇa entitled Bhāgavatam - "Tales of the All-Attractive" - which is a Vedic equivalent originally taught to Brahmā by the All-Attractive during the first day of Brahmā's life. By reciting these tales he would answer each and every inquiry put forward by the great King.

CHAPTER NINE:

THE ORIGINAL TALE

Śuka began by answering the king's question about the relationship between the soul and the body. "The soul," he said, "is a superior thing, full of its own natural consciousness. There is no factual relationship between it and the body. The apparent relationship is a byproduct of self-delusion, similar to the effect of identifying with characters in a dream."

"Why would the soul want to delude itself like this?" the king asked.

"Because it wants to enjoy the world," Śuka explained. "The soul wants to enjoy the world in many different ways, so it eventually identifies with many different forms - always deluding itself into the fantasy that each one is 'I' and 'mine.'"

"Can the soul get free from this self-delusion?" the king asked.

"Yes," Śuka answered. "The soul can become free from false delusions of 'I' and 'mine' as soon as it ceases to seek enjoyment the world and instead develops the desire enjoy its own timeless and factual inherent glory."

"What is the soul's timeless and factual inherent glory?" the king asked.

Śuka said that Brahmā received the answer to this question from the All-Attractive, whose direct and beautiful audience he obtained due to having worshipped him in a sincere way. He began to tell Brahmā's tale, in which the king would find profound answers to his many questions.

Brahmā's Search

In the beginning, Brahmā, the first god and supreme authority in the universe, was confused. Where did he come from? What should he do? He couldn't figure out which way to go, nor how he should assemble any materials.

While he was in the celestial waters seeking out the root of his abode he heard two syllables being uttered not far away.

Soon after, he heard it again.

He heard the sixteenth and twenty-first syllables, counted by the system of how the mouth naturally tends to vocalize. These two syllables join together to form a word that is famous as the wealth of those who renounce all wealth. That word is tapa, austerity.

When he heard that word, he searched everywhere for the person who spoke it. but no matter where he looked he found no one except himself. "Someone seems to be advising me," he thought, "that it would be beneficial to perform austerity." So, he returned to his original place and set his mind to the task.

For a thousand celestial years, he applied his flawless intellect to controlling his breath, mind, and especially his incoming and outgoing senses. He fully applied himself to this very disciplined austerity, which would generate the power that could generate all the worlds; for, by seeing the sincerity of Brahmā's efforts, the All-Attractive became pleased to empower him.

In the process of empowering him, the All-Attractive completely revealed his own abode, the infinitely supreme realm, to Brahmā.

Brahmā's Darśan of Hari's Realm

Hari's realm is worthy of the constant and abundant praise of self-realized people. In it, Brahmā perceived that all sources of suffering, illusion, and fear were completely absent. Ambition and ignorance had no place there; they could not mix with its pure existence.[41] Time could not dominate and transform things, and thus limitations like delusion could not arise.

Every being in that realm is dedicated to the will of Hari, and is worshipable by the greatest divine or demonic powers of this common world.

The men there are brilliantly dark-blue. Their eyes expand like hundred-petaled lotuses. Their very ornamental clothing glistens with brilliant golden colors. They all have four arms and wear radiant golden medallions along with earrings, crowns, and necklaces of unsurpassable and brilliant pearls, corals, cat's-eye, and blooming lotuses.

The exceedingly alluring and attractive damsels there have bright golden complexions. When these effulgent souls travel with the dark-blue men in clusters of sparkling airships it seems like lightning flashing amidst thick clouds.

The most beautiful among all these women is Śrī. She expands her powers into a plurality of goddesses, and together they give their full attention to serving the feet of Hari in many different ways. Their favorite service is to sit with Hari on a swing while the humming and buzzing of bumblebees accompanies their singing of the beloved deeds of he whose feet are the subject of the best of songs.

In the midst of those goddesses, Brahmā saw the All-Powerful husband of Śrī, the husband of all pure souls, the husband of all who sacrifice, the husband of all that exists, who is served in all ways by his companions[42] and leans

---

[41] *Rajas* and *tamas* did not exist, they could not blend with the pure *sattva*.

[42] Companions specifically mentioned here: Sunanda, Nanda, Prabala, and Arhaṇa

affectionately towards his servants, who are drunk from the liquor of seeing him. The dawn of a soothing smile decorates his eyes and face, while a crown and earrings glitter like Venus in that dawn. He has four arms, is dressed in yellow, and his chest is marked by Śrī.

Seated on a throne of utmost adoration, surrounded by his four, sixteen and five energies,[43] empowered with his inherent opulences as well as the minor opulences of any other entity, the Master thoroughly delights in his own abode.[44]

This vision flooded Brahmā's soul with bliss. His hair stood on end and tears of love poured from his eyes. He, the creator of the universe, bowed to Hari's lotus-like feet, which are the final destination on the path followed by the supreme spiritualists. When Hari saw so much divine love filling this enlightened scientist, he considered Brahmā competent to serve his will in creating and populating the universe. The endearer touched the endeared with his very loving hand and began to speak enlightening words with a succulent smile.

The All-Attractive said:

---

[43] Śrīla Viśvanātha's commentary explains: **Four** refers to (a) the opulences: *dharma, jñāna, aiśvarya,* and *vairāgya*, (b) the powers of existence: *prakṛti, puruṣa, mahat,* and *ahaṁkāra,* or (c) the powers of the four Veda. **Sixteen** refers to (a) the sixteen doorkeepers and directional guardians of Vaikuṇṭha, or (b) the sixteen principles that expand from the four energies of existence: ten senses + five elements + the mind. **Five** refers to (a) the five energies that sustain Vaikuṇṭha: Kūrma, Ananta, Garuḍa, the Vedic hymns, and Vedic *mantras*, or (b) the five essences of sense perception: sight, sound, touch, taste, and scent. The "(b)" set was initially given by Śrīdhara Swāmī. They show that the material energy is also sheltered and rooted in Vaikuṇṭha, although they cannot exhibit their energies in that realm.

[44] "**Inherent opulences**:" Wealth, strength, fame, beauty, wisdom, and detachment. The "**minor opulences**" show that Hari permanently and fully possesses every attractive feature that any other living entity might temporarily exhibit. "**Delights in his own abode**" shows Hari is unlike bewildered entities who try to enjoy extrinsic, external objects. He enjoys internal objects, expansions of his own intrinsic being.

"Even the most extreme yogis find it very difficult to satisfy me, but I am completely satisfied by you! Let the long austerities you've performed impregnate you with all the knowledge required to create the universe! Brahmā, be blessed! I am the master of wish-fulfillment, so please ask me for anything you wish."

Aware of the purity of Brahmā's ecstatic heart, Hari added, "Yes, I can even grant the ultimate success: my own direct company."

Seeing Brahmā shy to request anything on his own behalf, Hari encouraged him by revealing that he has always been fulfilling Brahmā's needs and desires. "I am the one who made your dearest wish come true by allowing you to see me in my own realm," he explained. "When you were all alone and had no idea what to do, you thought you heard a voice. That was my voice! Inspired by it, you performed your excellent self-discipline. By this self-discipline you won my heart and soul. And so, I want to empower you to create the contents of the universe. I can give you this power because I possess it myself. By the power of my own absolute self-discipline I create this existence. By the power of self-discipline, I then destroy it. By the power of self-discipline I maintain it all."

Brahmā's Requests

Brahmā replied: "You are within everyone's heart. You know every secret. You know our every desire with unimpeded clarity. Nonetheless you provide necessities to those who express their needs, so I will express the wishes you already know I cherish."

Hari's satisfied smile bloomed ever more delightfully.

Brahmā's first wish: "You are beyond form, yet have form - in both a natural and supernatural context. I want to fully comprehend this."

His second wish: "You are completely independent, self-sufficient and self-made, yet your magic combines with its own various potencies to destroy, create, accept and maintain everything. I want to fully comprehend this."

His third: "Like a spider expanding a web, your flawless will expands honey-sweet playful pastimes. Please grant me an intellect that can fully comprehend them."

Finally, he added, "I want to be an instrument of your will to create beings, but please be kind to me and do not let me become bewildered by such powerful deeds. Allow me to assist you the creation of all sorts of entities, O Lord. Bless me to immerse myself in doing your business without being disturbed by entertaining the madness that I am equal to you, my Beginningless Master, even though you affectionately treat me like a friend."

With great pleasure, Hari replied, "Try to grasp what I will now explain. I will describe esoteric practices that reveal the most confidential secrets you wish to comprehend about my dimensions, potencies, forms, qualities and deeds. My compassion will empower you to fully realize it all."

Singular and Plural

Hari began his first instruction: "Only I exclusively exist - at the very beginning, at the end, and throughout the duration of everything else."

Brahmā asked, "What is 'everything else'?"

"Every cause," Hari said, "and every effect."

Brahmā asked, "You say there is 'something else' but you also say that everything is you. Please clarify this."

"I am the causeless cause of all causes," Hari explained, "the beginningless beginning of all beginnings, the exclusive existence existing before, after and during everything else. All that exists is me."

"Is that what you mean by the word exclusively?" Brahmā asked.

"Yes," Hari replied, "I alone exist. This means that I exist without dependence on any other circumstance. I am the self-manifesting experience of blissful existence. I alone am the effect that causes itself. I alone am beyond all cause and effect."

"In the very beginning," Brahmā asked, "are you literally all alone? Are you originally a singular substance without the plurality of names, forms, qualities, and actions?

"It can be said that I was singular," Hari replied, "but actually all pluralities of individuality eternally exist within my singular existence."

Brahmā asked, "If you are the only factual being existing before, after and during everything - then everything we see and everything we don't see is actually you?"

"Yes," Hari admitted. "My natural form is everything you will see during the manifestation of the universe. My supernatural form is what cannot be seen within the universe. It is beyond cause and effect, existing before the beginning and after the end of everything else."

Real and Unreal

Hari then began his second instruction: "My magic," he said, "can make the unreal seem real, and the real seem unreal. It hides reality from anyone whose heart dislikes it, granting unreal perceptions instead. Thus I create the unreal world of illusion."

"How do you manifest the real world?" Brahmā asked.

"My magic," Hari explained, "can also reveal the truth of real things and the falsity of unreal things. Thus I manifest the real world for those whose hearts are inclined towards reality."

Brahmā understood deeply. One spell of Hari's magic, a spell called māyā, manifests an illusory reality for those who desire it, within which divinity takes the form of material nature. Another spell of the same magic, a spell called yoga-māyā, manifests factual reality to those who desire it. Within this reality divinity manifests in supernatural, transcendental forms.

"These energies of mine," Hari continued, "don't just reveal the external objects of perception, they also reveal self-perception. Thus one spell of my magic hides the true identity and reveals a false one to those who so desire. Another spell, for those who embrace truth, hides any false individuality and reveals the true identity."

"Your magic," Brahmā said, "seems to be like light and darkness, simultaneously."

"Yes!" Hari enthusiastically agreed. "My magic is like light because it reveals things to the consciousness. When light shines directly on an object, you see it as it is. But when light glares nearby, the object is cast into shadow and cannot be perceived as it is. Darkness is made all the more impenetrable by a dazzling glare nearby, misdirecting ones focus and contracting the pupil. Thus the light of my magic can both reveal and hide reality; it can both create and dispel illusions."

Within and Beyond

Hari then began his third instruction: "I am within all realities," he said, "yet outside them, too."

"Can you give an example," Brahmā asked, "to help me comprehend this apparent contradiction?"

"Yes," Hari replied. "Take the elements for example. The primordial elements of the universe are beyond everything within the universe, yet they are also within everything in the universe, great and small, because everything has evolved from them. Similarly I am beyond yet within all perceptions of reality."

"What are the ramifications of this?" Brahmā asked.

"I am spread throughout all of reality," Hari explained, "But because I am also beyond reality, I can localize myself and display my individual name, form, qualities, and activities. Although I am within all things, I also have my own transcendent individuality distinct from them.

"Although the truth is that I am everywhere," Hari continued, "my presence is not tangibly obvious within the illusory realm. Only in the factual realm am I tangibly and directly perceived as I am. Being 'within yet beyond' also means that I am within one of my magic spells, but beyond the other."

Hari explained the phrase further, "'I am within all things,' this means that I invest some portion of myself into all things, but, 'I am beyond all things,' means that I am not fully invested into everything. I am everywhere in all realities, but I am very detached from the affairs of illusory realities. In that arena I merely facilitate everyone's dreams of independence and self-importance, in an utterly neutral and dispassionate manner. On the other hand I am wholly and passionately engrossed in true reality. I wholeheartedly and emotionally give myself to the entities within that reality." Hari put his quivering hand to his heart as tears welled in his eyes. "I offer my divine beauty," he said, "simply to serve their divine vision, decorating myself and dancing for them. I offer the divine sound of my flute and my voice to their divine hearing, playing music that delights them, and playfully conversing with them day and night. I drift into their noses as my intoxicating fragrance. I enwrap their skin with my velvet-silk embrace. And I fill their mouths with the nectar flavor of my kisses. So, my heart is detached from the affairs of illusion, yet passionately attached to the affairs of reality."

Directly and Indirectly

Hari then began his fourth and final instruction: "If you want to fully realize these truths I've described, certainly you must eagerly investigate them to the fullest extent!"

"How?" Brahmā asked.

"By inquiring. Always be inquisitive," Hari answered.

"But who should I inquire from?" Brahmā asked.

"From individuals," Hari said, "who have themselves comprehended these truths."

"How did they realize these truths?" Brahmā asked.

"By their own inquiry and investigation," Hari replied.

"Who did they inquire from?" Brahmā asked.

"They inquired from those who inquired before them," Hari replied.

"Is this chain of inquiry infinite," Brahmā asked, "or does it have an origin?"

"I am the origin," Hari said. "It is only by my mercy that anyone can comprehend anything about me, who am beyond everyone. My mercy spreads out in the world through those who have already availed themselves of it. To realize spiritual truths, inquire from one who has already realized, guru. This chain of inquiry carries my merciful blessing which makes it possible for the infinitesimal to comprehend the infinite."

"How should I inquire?" Brahmā asked.

"Always and everywhere," Hari answered. "Directly and indirectly."

The phrase always and everywhere, indicates that no one is disqualified from discovering Hari, and no situation exists in which Hari cannot be discovered. It also indicates that inquisitiveness about Hari is eternal and thus the essence of this adventure does not cease, even when one has gone beyond imperfection.

Direct inquiry includes questions like, "What am I? What is reality?" Indirect inquiry includes questions like, "What is not me? What is not reality?" We must directly inquire by seeking to understand the value of divine love, for example; and indirectly inquire by seeking to understand the worthlessness of not having divine love. Direct inquiry also indicates the quest to taste divine love in union with Hari, while indirect inquiry indicates the search for the taste of divine love in separation from him.

Extremely emotional, Brahmā said, "I am so joyful to hear your eloquent explanations of transcendental truth. But I am afraid I will lose this joyful consciousness, this intimate connection with you, when you depart and I turn my attention to my mighty business as the creator."

Hari leaned towards Brahmā affectionately and replied, "I bless you: you will always remain fixed in this supreme concentration upon Reality. Throughout the many eras of your long life, this realization you now possess will never completely dissolve into illusion."

Having thus completely edified the supreme leader of living beings, beginningless Hari withdrew the visibility of his beautiful self.

Brahmā's Dearest Son, Nārada

When the most treasured object of perception withdrew, Brahmā very respectfully joined his palms. He then set his mind to creating all the entities in the universe, as they once were. As the father of everyone, he desired to create auspiciousness for his children. So he set a fatherly example of how to satisfy one's desires by governing oneself according to moral rules and regulations.

Nārada followed his father's example of self-control very humbly, deeply, sincerely, and scrupulously. Thus he became Brahmā's dearest child. Nārada was very scholarly, very devotional, and very inquisitive to learn about the potencies of Viṣṇu, the master of all potency. That's why he tried so hard to completely satisfy his father. When he felt that his father was pleased, he placed many questions before Brahmā, just like the questions you have asked me, O King.

The creator of beings, Brahmā, affectionately answered all these questions by explaining what All-Attractive Hari had taught him. Thus, the Beautiful Tales of the All-Attractive began to take shape, with ten subjects. Nārada would later explain it all to the unlimitedly powerful scholar, Vyāsa, who meditated upon the Supreme Spirit, on the shore of Sarasvatī River.

Śuka told King Parīkṣit, "I learned these tales from Vyāsa. By explaining them to you, I will answer all your questions, beginning with how this universe is related to the Original Person."

Chapter Ten:

The Ultimate Refuge

"You said that these Beautiful Tales have ten subjects," the king asked, "What are they?"

Śuka explained that they were essentially the same ten subjects about which the king had just inquired. He enumerated them:

Origin (*sarga*)

Creation (*visarga*)

Existence (*sthāna*)

Maintenance (*poṣaṇa*)

Deeds (ūti)

Spans of Time (*manvantara*)

Discussion of the Devotees (*īśa-anu kathā*)

Destruction (*nirodha*)

Liberation (*mukti*)

The Ultimate Refuge (*āśraya*)

The tenth is the main subject. The first nine clarify its true meaning. Great spiritualists narrate and elaborate on these ten subjects, by quoting what they have heard from scripture and explaining it clearly and directly.

"Please briefly explain each subject," the king requested.

"The first subject is ***sarga*** - Origin," Śuka explained. "It is about how elements, perceptibility, perception, and intellect originate from the spiritual substance when it's qualities are unbalanced.

"The second subject is ***visarga*** - Creation. It is about how individual entities come into being, as specific combinations of elements, perceptions, and so on.

"The third subject is ***sthāna*** - Existence. By describing the state of existence in the created world, it reveals the superiority of the spiritual world.

"The fourth subject is ***poṣaṇa*** - Maintenance. By describing the efforts he exerts to maintain the existence of the created world, it reveals how affectionately merciful the Tranquil Victor is.

"The fifth subject is ***ūti*** - Deeds. By describing the destinations attainable through various efforts, it reveals how desires implicate us in a causal chain, karma.

"The sixth subject is ***manvantara*** - Spans of Time. By discussing historical time spans, it reveals the good conduct of outstanding leaders.

"The seventh subject is ***īśa-anu-kathā*** - Discussions of the Devotees. It includes many tales about the incarnations of Hari and, of course, the devotional deeds of their devotees.

"The eighth subject is ***nirodha*** - Destruction. This is about how all individuals and energies fall into slumber when Hari lies down.

"The ninth subject is ***mukti*** - Liberation. It describes how a living being can cast off all extraneous forms of identity and permanently acquire his or her constitutional identity and form.

"The tenth subject is ***āśraya*** - The Ultimate Refuge. It describes the entity who is the ultimate source of both manifestation and dissolution, the Supreme Spirit, the Supreme Soul."

Is The Soul The Ultimate Refuge?

"What is the difference," Parīkṣit asked, "between the soul and the Supreme Soul?"

"The soul is the refuge of three treasures," Śuka explained, "but is not its own refuge."

"What are those three treasures?" the king asked.

Śuka replied, "the three treasures sheltered in the sanctuary of the soul are individuality, divinity, and substance."[45]

"Please explain each one," the king requested.

"Individuality defines a person," Śuka explained, "as a specific instance of divine powers. Substance is what stands between the two."

"I don't understand," the king admitted.

Śuka clarified. "Individuality is tangible as consciousness - the awareness of things from a particular point of view. Divinity is tangible as the power of perception - the superior position of observer rather than the observed. Substance is tangible as the senses of a physical body."

"How does the body," Parīkṣit asked, "'stand between' consciousness and perception?"

Śuka explained, "In one sense this means that the body is a conduit for consciousness and perception, an interface between the two. In another sense it means the body is a divider, a blockage between the two, because investing individuality into an unreal substance cuts us off from divinity."

---

[45] *Adhyātmika, adhidaivika, adhibhautika*

Now that the king understood the three treasures sheltered in the soul, he asked, "Why is the soul not its own refuge? What is the soul's refuge?"

Śuka explained, "The three qualities cannot shelter themselves because their existence is relative to and dependent upon one another. If one is absent, the others cannot manifest. Thus as a unit they must be sheltered, anchored, in some fourth entity. That entity is the soul, the true individual. The soul can therefore possess and utilize all three treasures. But the soul is not self-sufficient, it is dependent on a fifth entity, the Supreme Soul. So, three treasures are sheltered in the soul, and the soul is sheltered by the Supreme Soul. The Supreme Soul is self-sufficient, his own shelter. Thus the ultimate refuge of everything is the Supreme Soul."

The Creation Before Creation

Śuka began answering the king's specific questions, by clarifying the relationship between the universe and the Original Person from whom it emanates.[46]

"The Original Person," he said, "separated the universal egg from himself. Yet in a pure, unentangled way he also remained within it. There, he wanted a place to lie down, so he manifest the purest water. That is why we call him Nārāyaṇa. We call him nara ("person") because he is the original person. We describe the pure universal waters as nāra ("from the person") because they came from that original person. We add the word ayana ("repose") because the Original Person rests upon the waters that come from him.

[46] The king had asked whether the Universal Form is a product of the Universe or visa versa.

"He rested in that water for one thousand years," Śuka continued, "absorbed in the primal creation to evolve the fundamental material elements, causality, time, psychology, and most importantly the conscious souls. All these are dependent upon him: They can manifest their reality when he is inclined towards them, but when he is disinclined they become unmanifest.

"The One desired to be many, so he arose from his own bed and injected his effulgently golden, divine potency into his illusory magic. Eventually, three offspring would be produced: the powers of perception, individuality, and substance. I will explain to you the evolution of this gestation.

"The Puruṣa accepts three distinct forms," Śuka continued. "one of them is the Universal Form you asked about. The Universal Form is the template of the universe," he said. "Everything that exists in the universe exists because it is a part of the template established by the Universal Form."

Śuka then elaborated fully on the gestational evolution of the Universal Form.

He explained that first there was only space within the Universal Form. From that space, the Puruṣa effortlessly generated three forces: sensual acuity, intellectual mastery, and physical strength.[47] Then he generated prāṇa, the all-important breath, to link and coordinate the three. That's why prāṇa is often called sūtra (thread). Prāṇa is absolutely essential. While it moves, we move, we live. When it stops, we stop, we die. Prāṇa is like a king and the three energies are like his soldiers.

The breath of life revealed digestion and thus generated hunger and thirst, which cause a mouth to differentiate itself in the Universal Form. The sense of taste then appeared within the mouth, generating the tongue, which generated the various flavors the tongue can enjoy.

---

[47] Sensual acuity *(ojaḥ)* is the energy of perception *(adhidaiva)*. Intellectual mastery *(sahaḥ)* is the energy of individuality *(adhyātma)*. Physical strength *(balam)* is the energy of substances *(adhibhūta)*.

The mouth of the Universal Form also wanted to speak, so the divinity of conversation generated the organs of speech and the meaningful sounds they produce.[48]

But he couldn't eat or speak because he was submerged in the water for a long, long time. So, the life-air within him began to flow, causing a nose to differentiate itself in the Universal Form. Taking a breath, he emerged from the waters desiring to experience smell. The divinity of air generated the sense of smell within his nose, along with all the fragrances carried by the air.[49]

The desire to see himself and other things then caused eyes to differentiate in the Universal Form. The divinity of light generated the sense of vision and the objects whose qualities it can grasp.[50]

Then, the desire to awaken and understand caused ears to differentiate in the Universal Form. The divinity of distance generated the sense of hearing and the objects whose qualities it can grasp.[51]

He wanted to experience the softness and hardness, lightness and heaviness, warmth and coolness in the tangible things he could see, hear, and smell, so a covering of skin with many fine hairs sprouting from pores differentiated in the Universal Form.[52] Through the divinity of wind, this skin

---

[48] The "divinity of conversation" is Vahni, the vehicle which conveys things from one entity to another. The divinities mentioned in this section are primordial, transcendental principles which also manifest later in cosmic evolution as one or more specific deities. Vahni mainly became analogous to the goddess of speech, Vāk, and the god of fire, Agñi. Fire allows conversation between the physical and energetic realms. It converts objects from physical to energetic states, allowing them to be conveyed from mortals to the immortals.

[49] The "divinity of air" is Vāyu.

[50] The "divinity of light" is Jyoti, analogous to the later demigods of visible light coming from the Sun.

[51] The "divinity of distance" is Diśa.

[52] The words used to express "many fine hairs sprouting from pores" also indicates foliage. The trees with the wind moving through them are directly analogous to the template of the fine hairs on the skin sensing the touch via the movement of air.

and hair acquired the internal and external sense of touch, and the objects whose qualities it can enjoy.[53]

Two hands sprouted from the Universal Body because of his desire to interact with things. The divinity of lordship empowered the hands with the power to seize and manipulate.[54]

Two feet sprouted from the Universal Body as a result of his special desire for movement. The deity of endeavor personally empowered the legs with the ability to move about, enabling beings to performing various deeds s sacrifices to the Universal Person.[55]

A penis certainly differentiated itself on the Universal Body, as a result of the endeavor for immortality and the desire to experience the bliss of procreation. The deity of procreation generated the counterpart genital, the vulva, and the two things required to enjoy sexual pleasure: desire and affection.[56]

Also, an anus certainly differentiated itself on the Universal Body as a result of the desire to expel unnecessary things. Through the divinity of holding, the anus acquired the two abilitics it depends on: expelling waste objects while holding important objects within.[57]

A door to the abdomen opened in the Universal Body when he desired to move from one body to another. Then the divinity of death generated the two things required for

---

[53] The "divinity of wind" is Vāṭa. There is a slight distinction between wind/Vāṭa and air/Vāyu, the former is the air that blows across our skin, enabling the sense of touch, the later is the air that we breathe into our lungs through our mouth and nose, enabling the sense of smell.
[54] The "deity of lordship" is Indra, later analogous to the Lord of Paradise.
[55] The "deity of endeavor" is Yajña, the force of sacrifice later analogous to Viṣṇu.
[56] The "divinity of procreation" is Praja, or Prajāpati, later analogous to the demigods who populate the universe.
[57] The "divinity of holding" is Mitra, the force which holds the sky separate from the earth, later analogous to the demigod of bonds and friendships.

transmigration: depression of breath, and separation of body and mind.[58]

The desire for food and drink also caused an abdominal cavity, intestines, and a circulatory system to exist. The rivers and seas then came into being, to supply the objects upon which satisfaction of hunger and satiation of thirst depend.[59]

The desire to contemplate his own illusions caused a "heart" to differentiate. Within the heart, the divinity of illumination generated the mind, with its two functions: opinions and desires.[60]

All of these senses organize and assemble themselves into a coherent and enduring bodily structure via seven substances: external skin, internal skin, muscle, blood, fat, marrow, and bone. The primal elements earth, water and fire manifest in the Universal Form to create these seven substances. The remaining two primal elements, space and air, manifest and combine with moisture to create the life-breath. These eight primal elements also wrap the Universal Form like layers of clothing.

Śuka also explained the primary function of each member of the Universal Form. "The purpose of ego," he said, "is to incline the consciousness towards attraction to manipulating the qualities of nature. The purpose of the senses is to perceive and interact with those qualities. The mind's purpose is to generate emotional content relative to those perceptions. The intellect's purpose is to comprehend all this.

---

[58] The "door to the abdomen" seems to primarily be the navel. It can be thought of as the portal out of one body and into the next. The "divinity of death" is Mṛtyu.

[59] The rivers and seas are divinities in Vedic thought. They provide water to satiate the thirst and irrigate the land to provide vegetation which satiates the hunger.

[60] The "divinity of illumination" is Candra, analogous to the later demigod of the moon. There is a slight distinction between the illumination of Jyoti and the illumination of Candra. Jyoti is an external light that enables sight. Candra is an inner light that enables inner vision.

"Beyond this," Śuka continued, "lies something supremely subtle: an unmanifest, undefined substance beyond the reach of words or thoughts, that eternally exists without beginning, middle, or end. This unmanifest substance and the manifest Universal Form are both manifestations of the All-Attractive, that is certain. But still, wise souls don't embrace either of them - since they are both creations of illusion."

King Parīkṣit asked, "What forms of the All-Attractive do the wise embrace?"

"They who are truly fit to speak of him," Śuka answered, "describe the All-Attractive in purely spiritual form beyond everything, yet perceivable with a specific name and shape. His actions are beyond cause and effect, yet he performs amazing deeds."

The king asked, "What relationship does such a transcendent entity have with this transient universe?"

"An indirect one," Śuka answered. "He expands into and empowers other living entities, especially Brahmā, to create a relative world in which consciousness becomes burdened with limited names, forms, and actions."

Brahmā's Creation

"What names and forms did Brahmā create in this world?" asked the king.

"He created the Prajāpatīs," Śuka answered. "Through them, he created the Manu (forbearers of mankind), the Deva (gods), the Ṛṣi (sages, especially the original seven), and the Pitṛ ("forefathers" who inhabit the netherworld); the Siddha, Cāraṇa, Gandharva, and Vidyādhara (super-humans with extreme mastery of fine arts and sciences); the Asura (demons) and Guhyaka (guardians of the netherworld's wealth); the Kinnara (animal-human hybrids), Apsara (masters of beauty, dance, and eros), Nāga (humanlike supernatural serpents), Sarpa (snakelike supernatural serpents), Kimpuruṣa (monkey-human hybrids), Nara (humans), and the Mātṛ ("foremothers" who inhabit the netherworld).

"Brahmā also created monstrous entities," Śuka continued, "like the Rakṣa (primal nature-spirits), Piśāca (ogres), Preta (undead), Bhūta (ghosts), Vināyaka (thievish goblins), Kūṣmāṇḍa (globular spirits that possess entities), Unmāda (lunatics), Vetāla (vampires), Yātudhas (man-eaters), and Graha (spirits that possess humans). He also created sub-human species like birds, wild animals, domestic animals, plants, crystals, and reptiles.

"He created every form of life in either of the two divisions (moving or not), or four divisions (those born from cellular division, seeds, eggs, or wombs), dwelling everywhere in the water, on land, or in the sky.

"All of the creatures created by Brahmā," Śuka concluded, "experience a mixture of fortune and misfortune as a result of their own actions."

The king wanted to know if there was a good way to organize all these different life forms into categories. Śuka explained that a life-form can be categorized according to its natural quality. The quality of clarity (sattva) generates heavenly species. The quality of ambition (rajas) generates humanoids. The quality of darkness (tamas) generates hellish species. Within each category are subcategories. By dividing each of the three natures into three sub-natures we can distinguish nine categories of species. This subdivision can continue into the fine gradations which account for the unique nature of each individual entity.

"Usually," the king asked, "We hear of Brahmā as one of three gods. What roles do the other two play?"

"All-Attractive Viṣṇu takes the form of dharma," Śuka replied, "to sustain, nourish, and fortify all the animals, humans, and gods in the universe.[61] He is also Rudra, who

---

[61] *Dharma* means essential nature. Fidelity to one's essential nature constitutes "morality," thus the word is often defined as such. A husband, for example, practices morality by being faithful to the duties born from

destroys his own creations in the fires of time, just like the wind annihilates the clouds.

"Brahmā, Rudra, and Viṣṇu are aspects of the All-Attractive," Śuka concluded, "but they exist only in relation to this illusory world. The divine lovers of the All-Attractive can see, with their higher vision, that the All-Attractive is beyond the illusory world, and not really involved with it. They never teach that the Transcendent Being is directly involved in material deeds like creation and so forth. He has absolutely no direct interest in authoring illusions. His illusory energy performs such tasks on its own."

"How often does creation occur?" the king asked.

Śuka answered, "Visnu's creation takes place at the beginning of Brahmā's life. Brahmā's sub-creation takes place at beginning of each of Brahmā's days. I'll eventually explain how to measure the duration and identify the characteristics of time-spans like the days of Brahmā. Let me begin by telling you about Brahmā's day called the Pādma-kalpa."[62]

What about Vidura?

The sages of Naimiśāraṇya listened carefully as Sūta recounted this tale of King Parīkṣit's conversation with Śuka. At the moment, they weren't particularly eager to hear about measurements of time. They wanted to hear instead about outstanding devotion and devotees. So Śaunaka voiced a question.

---

his essential nature as the protector and benefactor of his wife. Animals faithfully abide by their inherent, instinctual natures. This fidelity to their essential nature is "*dharma*" and it protects, sustains, and nourishes them.

[62] *Padma-kalpa* = "Lotus timespan."

"O Sūta," Śaunaka inquired, "you kindly mentioned that Vidura, a man of mixed-birth but a topmost lover of the All-Attractive, did something very difficult: he left his friends and relatives and journeyed to sacred places around the world. When Vidura met the sage Maitreya they had a deep discussion on spirituality. The blessed sage answered every question by speaking the truth. My dear, gracious boy, please tell us about this conversation, and also explain what caused Vidura to leave his friends and relatives, and what caused him to later return."

Sūta replied, "King Parīkṣit asked this same question to the great sage, Śuka. Please listen, I will explain the answer Śuka gave."

Acknowledgments

I am eternally and happily indebted to Śrīla A.C. Bhaktivedānta Swāmī Prabhupāda, who presented the original Sanskrit of the Beautiful Tales elaborately transliterated, translated, and explained. Similarly I am forever in the debt of those great souls past and present who's patient commentary and guidance reveals the self-effulgent brilliance of these tales. In particular I would like to express my gratitude to Śrīla Viśvanātha Cakravartī and to my personal mentors headed by Śrīmad Dhanurdhara Swāmī and Śrīmad Satyanārāyaṇa dāsa Bābājī.

Other Books by the Author

Beautiful Tales of the All-Attractive
(Śrīmad Bhāgavatam's First Canto)

Varāha, Vidura & Kapila
(Śrīmad Bhāgavatam's Third Canto)

A Simple Gītā

To Dance in the Downpour of Devotion

VrajaKishor.com

25269652R00069

Made in the USA
Middletown, DE
24 October 2015